T0366605

SELECTED
POEMS

BY ADRIENNE RICH

SELECTED
POEMS
1950–2012

ADRIENNE
RICH

EDITED AND WITH AN INTRODUCTION BY

Albert Gelpi, Barbara Charlesworth Gelpi, and Brett C. Millier

W. W. NORTON & COMPANY

Independent Publishers Since 1923

New York | London

Copyright © 2018, 2013 by the Adrienne Rich Literary Trust. Copyright © 2011, 2007, 2004, 2001, 1999, 1995, 1991, 1989, 1986, 1984, 1981, 1967, 1963, 1962, 1961, 1960, 1959, 1958, 1957, 1956, 1955, 1954, 1953, 1952, 1951 by Adrienne Rich. Copyright © 1984, 1978, 1975, 1973, 1971, 1969, 1966 by W. W. Norton & Company, Inc.
Introduction copyright © 2018 by Albert Gelpi, Barbara Charlesworth Gelpi, and Brett C. Millier

For information about permission to reproduce selections from this book, write to Permissions, W. W. Norton & Company, Inc., 500 Fifth Avenue, New York, NY 10110

For information about special discounts for bulk purchases, please contact W. W. Norton Special Sales at specialsales@wwnorton.com or 800-233-4830

Manufacturing by LSC Harrisonburg
Book design by Chris Welch Design
Production manager: Julia Druskin

Library of Congress Cataloging-in-Publication Data

Names: Rich, Adrienne, 1929–2012, author. | Gelpi, Albert, editor.
Title: Selected poems, 1950–2012 / Adrienne Rich ; edited by Albert Gelpi, Barbara Charlesworth Gelpi, and Brett C. Millier.
Description: First edition. | New York : W. W. Norton & Company, 2018.
Identifiers: LCCN 2018016676 | ISBN 9780393355116 (pbk.)
Classification: LCC PS3535.I233 A6 2018b | DDC 811/.54—dc23
LC record available at https://lccn.loc.gov/2018016676

W. W. Norton & Company, Inc., 500 Fifth Avenue, New York, N.Y. 10110
www.wwnorton.com

W. W. Norton & Company Ltd., 15 Carlisle Street, London W1D 3BS

4 5 6 7 8 9 0

CONTENTS

From *Snapshots of a Daughter-in-Law: Poems 1954–1962* (1963)

From *Necessities of Life: Poems 1962–1965* (1966)

From *Leaflets: Poems 1965–1968* (1969)

From *The Will to Change: Poems 1968–1970* (1971)

From *Diving into the Wreck: Poems 1971–1972* (1973)

From *Poems: Selected and New, 1950–1974* (1975)

From *The Dream of a Common Language:* *Poems 1974–1977* (1978)

From *A Wild Patience Has Taken Me This Far:* *Poems 1978–1981* (1981)

From *Your Native Land, Your Life: Poems* (1986)

From *Time's Power: Poems 1985–1988* (1989)

From *An Atlas of the Difficult World: Poems 1988–1991* (1991)

From *Dark Fields of the Republic:*
Poems 1991–1995 (1995)

From *Midnight Salvage: Poems 1995–1998* (1999)

From *Fox: Poems 1998–2000* (2001)

From *The School Among the Ruins:*
Poems 2000–2004 (2004)

From *Telephone Ringing in the Labyrinth:*
Poems 2004–2006 (2007)

From *Tonight No Poetry Will Serve: Poems*
2007–2010 (2011)

From *Later Poems:*
Selected and New, 1971–2012 (2013)

INTRODUCTION

I write out my life
hour by hour, word by word

—*"Incipience" (1971)*

Over a distinguished poetic career of more than sixty years Adrienne Rich became a powerful witnessing presence in American culture, a clear and undeniable voice addressing the crucial issues of her—and our—time and place. This generous selection from all her published books of poems demonstrates the force and range of her vision as well as the verbal and formal inventiveness that crafted witness into enduring art. "Change" is a key word, and the arc of Rich's poetic development can be charted by following her changing sense of change. Her first collection of poems was titled *A Change of World* (1951), and with her third collection, *Snapshots of a Daughter-in-Law* (1963), she began to fix a date to each poem and to subtitle her books with dates indicating the years covered in that collection. She wanted her readers to attend consciously to the fact that she was a poet acutely aware of living in time and history: "We're living through a time / that needs to be lived through us" ("The Will to Change").

"Living Memory" (1988) ends with these challenging lines: "Time's / power, the only just power—would you / give it away?" Rich titled the volume in which it appears *Time's Power*, and her declarative response to the pressures and responsibilities of living in time creates the body of work that is her immense achievement. The words "time," "year," "life," and "day"—with their variants: "lifetime," "today," "yearlong," and so on—occur hundreds of times in the poems. "Storm Warnings," the first poem in the first book, announces the overarching theme of her poems:

an existential crisis that is at once personal and cultural, psychological and moral. In the early poem "Air Without Incense" and in later poems like "Transcendental Etude" (1977), Rich explicitly forgoes any religious or metaphysical resolution to the problem of time. If the crisis is human and historical, then so must be the hope for a resolution: *A Change of World* requires *The Will to Change* (1971).

Adrienne Cecile Rich was born on May 16, 1929, in Baltimore, Maryland, the elder of two sisters (Cynthia was born in 1933). Her father, Arnold Rice Rich, was Alabama-born, a secular Jewish physician and educator who encouraged the precociously talented Adrienne in her literary ambitions and gave her access to his extensive library of canonical nineteenth-century poets. Her mother, Helen Jones Rich, was a southern Protestant concert pianist who ended her performing career with her marriage. Adrienne was educated at home until the fourth grade and then attended the Roland Park Country School, an Episcopal girls' preparatory school. In 1947, she entered Radcliffe College, graduating in 1951, noting later that in her English and writing coursework, she had encountered no female teachers. Her poetry career was launched in 1951, when her first collection, *A Change of World,* won the Yale Younger Poet's Prize, adjudicated and introduced by W. H. Auden. In 1952, with funding from her first Guggenheim Fellowship, she traveled in England and Italy. While abroad, she fell ill and was diagnosed with acute rheumatoid arthritis, an autoimmune disease she suffered from—enduring many surgeries and nearly continuous pain—for the rest of her life.

On June 26, 1953, against her parents' wishes, she married Alfred Haskell Conrad, a Jew from Brooklyn and a Harvard economics professor whom she had met in college, and she took on the role of faculty wife in Cambridge, Massachusetts. In the early years of her marriage, Rich continued to write and participated in the heady poetic atmosphere of Boston and Cambridge that centered on Robert Lowell and included Anne Sexton and Sylvia Plath. In Rich's first two books, poems like "At a Bach Concert" and "The Diamond Cutters" show that her initial response to the conflicted violence of contemporary existence is to recoil in baffled self-defense and contain its disorder by sublimating it into the structured hermeticism of art: world changed into poem. *The Diamond Cutters* appeared in March 1955, the same month she gave birth to David, the first of three sons. Pablo was born in 1957 and Jacob in 1959. "The experience of motherhood was eventually to radicalize me," Rich said later.

She continued to receive honors and fellowships from the cultural establishment—a National Institute of Arts and Letters Award (1960) and her second Guggenheim (1961). By the late fifties, however, her poetry had begun to change. At a poetry reading she gave in 1964, she described the basic shift in her poetics: "instead of poems *about* experiences I am getting poems that *are* experiences, that contribute to my knowledge and emotional life even while they reflect and assimilate it. . . . [I]n the more recent poems something is happening, something has happened to me and, if I have been a good parent to the poem, something will happen to you who read it." By changing both the poet and the reader, the poem can begin to make things happen and thus change the world. The trenchant title poem (1958–1960) of *Snapshots of a Daughter-in-Law* (1963) celebrates an emerging vision that is historical and political and (drawing out the repressed implications of earlier poems like "Aunt Jennifer's Tigers" and "An Unsaid Word") feminist. In discerning what it means to be a woman and a poet, she found Emily Dickinson both an inspiration and a warning, and in "The Roofwalker" (1961), dedicated to Denise Levertov, Rich sees herself breaking out of the constraints of house and home.

When Alfred Conrad joined the faculty of the City University of New York in 1966, Rich and her family left Cambridge and joined the political and poetic ferment of New York City. She began teaching in the new SEEK program at the university, designed to help underprivileged high school students prepare for college. Her deepening political consciousness and activism against the Vietnam War and against the oppressive structures of a capitalist system can be tracked in the poems of *Leaflets* (1969) and *The Will to Change*. And, for respite and renewal, she regularly retreated with her family to their northeastern Vermont farmhouse; this "old house in America" and its landscape figure in a number of her poems.

In the fall of 1970, Alfred Conrad's ongoing depression deepened, and he committed suicide. In the midst of her grief, Rich began to change again. She fell in love with a woman for the first time and became, as the decade of the seventies progressed, the most powerful poetic voice of second-wave feminism and specifically of lesbian feminism. Poems such as "Planetarium" (1968), "Diving into the Wreck" (1972), and "The Phenomenology of Anger" (1972) received national and international recognition and response; and *Of Woman Born* (1976), a political examination of the institution of motherhood, and the essays in *On Lies, Secrets, and Silence* (1979) and *Blood, Bread, and Poetry* (1984) announced Rich as a major feminist thinker and cultural critic as well. Her *Twenty-One Love Poems* (1974–1976) reflects on the joy, difficulty, and painful end of a lesbian relationship. Later in 1976, she met the Jamaican-American writer Michelle Cliff, and they became partners for more than thirty-six years, until Rich's death.

Rich has been best known for the feminist poems of *Diving into the Wreck* (1973) and *The Dream of a Common Language* (1978), but in fact her politics continued to evolve. She began to read deeply in the writings of Karl Marx and in Marxist cultural criticism. In the foreword to the essays in *Arts of the Possible* (2001), Rich summed up her political development: a "fusion of Marx's humanism with contemporary feminisms expanded my sense of the possibilities of both." Mindful always of her audience, she adds, "I have been a poet of oppositional imagination, meaning that I don't think my only argument is with myself" but also "for people who want to imagine and claim wider horizons."

As Rich began to see gender bias more clearly as inextricably intertwined with discrimination by race and economic class, the poems of the 1980s began to widen politically and even geographically. In books like *Your Native Land, Your Life* (1986), *An Atlas of the Difficult World* (1991), and *Dark Fields of the Republic* (1995), the feminist poet became the witness to the nation, the first American woman to assume that poetic role. She looked back to Walt Whitman and Robinson Jeffers as American prophets, but, in "Yom Kippur 1984," she rejected Jeffers' individualist isolation in favor of Whitman's democratic populism at the same time that she found in the poet Muriel Rukeyser a kindred spirit closer to her time and place.

In her later career, Rich taught English and writing at several colleges and universities, including Columbia, Rutgers, and Stanford, and was a visiting writer or fellowship holder at several more. She remained an active and innovative poet and essayist throughout her life, producing a half-dozen more volumes of verse and four essay collections. She continued to receive prizes and awards, including a National Endowment for the Arts Fellowship in 1970, the National Book Award (1974) for *Diving into the Wreck*, a MacArthur Fellowship (1994), and the Bollingen Prize (2003). Rich and Cliff moved to California in 1984 and lived for nearly twenty-five years in Santa Cruz, where Rich died of complications from rheumatoid arthritis on March 27, 2012.

POETRY IS A temporal art, and a poet living in time lives, in a very real sense, in the measured rhythms of the poetic line and stanza. Organically over the years of her long career, Rich's poetics and poetic practice thus changed and evolved with her politics. Like her contemporaries Robert Lowell and John Berryman, she was trained in the metrical formalism of the New Criticism institutionalized in mid-twentieth-century universities; the assumed lyric voice expressed its private anxieties and ironies in iambs and rhyme. The models in her Harvard milieu were Robert Frost and Wallace Stevens. But, like Lowell and

Berryman, she found her own ways, starting in the *Snapshots* volume, to free herself into more open and angular forms. The restless, probing rhythms, the words and images with cutting edges and urgent energy spoke in a voice now unmistakably her own. However, as her politics widened, the poems tended more and more to extend their scope and length; they ran to sequences that included other voices and presences: from "The Burning of Paper Instead of Children" (1968) and "From an Old House in America" (1974) to later sequences, peopled with Whitmanesque catalogs and vignettes, as in "An Atlas of the Difficult World" (1990–1991), "Calle Visión" (1992–1993), "Midnight Salvage" (1996), and "Powers of Recuperation" (2007).

At the same time, Rich's comment on an argument "with myself," quoted above, alludes to W. B. Yeats' dictum that "we make out of the quarrel with others, rhetoric, and out of the quarrel with ourselves, poetry." Even as she spoke to and with and for others, her argument began as and remained an argument with herself; she knew that for effective change politics must be grounded and tested in the lived time of personal experience. Indeed, what makes her voice unmistakable is the fact that the public voice is inseparable from the private voice.

Nonetheless, the private voice is often not as immediately audible as the public one. Although the familial reference in the title of *Snapshots of a Daughter-in-Law* might carry the suggestion that Rich numbered herself among the "confessional" poets of the period—such as Robert Lowell, John Berryman, Sylvia Plath, and Anne Sexton—she strongly and consistently resisted that focus on the merely personal, just as she resisted the many overtures she received from potential biographers. In this connection consider two epigraphs to *Telephone Ringing in the Labyrinth* (2007). Rich quotes an observation by Michael S. Harper, who is himself quoting Sterling A. Brown: "Poetry is not self-expression, the I is a dramatic I." Then comes a further statement: "To which I would add: and so, unless otherwise indicated, is the You. A.R."

Like Joyce's artist, these sentences suggest, the poet is "within or behind or beyond his handiwork" but is not engaged in self-disclosure or dialogue with an actual interlocutor. Yet what are we to make of the qualifying phrase "unless otherwise indicated"? There are times, we are given to understand, when the "You" *is* a designated person with a very specific relationship to the "I" of the poem. And in such circumstances the "I" also necessarily becomes in turn a relational signifier for an "A.R." at a particular historical (and also biographical) time and place, connected in powerful ways to the "You" being addressed.

Often for Rich—indeed, perhaps, more often than not—personal pronouns are bearers of a trans- and interpersonal experience. An example is the soaring, deep-diving description of the "We," "I," and "you" who "find our way / back to this scene" at the conclusion of "Diving into the Wreck." However, at the conclusion of the sequence *Twenty-One Love Poems*, something quite different occurs. While not made up of the sonnets traditional in sequences such as Sydney's *Astrophel and Stella* or Elizabeth Browning's *Sonnets from the Portugese*, *Twenty-One Love Poems* has the traditional subject matter: a love story, albeit one that sets up a new tradition in that the passion described is between two women. Also, as is traditional, the beloved, though serving as inspiration for the poems, remains a presence rather than a specific and identifiable person. In poem XVIII, however, with a strategy designed for the shock effect it achieves, the line "where I am Adrienne alone" cites the first name of a poet living in a particular time and individual circumstances and thereby changes a poetic, (paradoxically) impersonal "I" into the signifier for a person. As a result, the "I" used in the last line of the sequence—"I choose to walk here"—confronts us with an unexpected, challenging, yet also deeply affecting, presence: the poet herself.

Rich uses the juxtaposition of her first name with the first-person singular of the speaking subject to create a similar immediacy but a different effect in numbers 6 and 7 of "Contradictions: Tracking Poems" (1983–1985). Like other poems of the divided self—Tennyson's "The Two Voices" or Yeats' "Dialogue of Self and Soul," for instance—these two poems turn on the poet's mission and are written during the years when Rich's sense of her role as a poet was changing. But she frames them as letters between two aspects of her named self, Adrienne. The rational, goal-oriented, productive Adrienne writes in number 6 that "I hope you have some idea / about the rest of your life"; the embodied, suffering Adrienne of poem number 7, responds: "But I'm already living the rest of my life . . . / wired   into pain / rider on the slow train." The use of her own name creates the sense of urgency, the struggle with despair, underlying the poems, while the brisk, ironic epistolary form avoids any trace of self-pity.

"You" is also often a dramatic, not a truly personal pronoun in Rich's work. Within the context of section 14 of "From an Old House in America," the "you" appears to be a man—"*what will you undertake* / she said"—but not a particular man. Still, on many occasions, with startling force, one realizes that this "you" is not general. Section 5 of "From an Old House in America" opens with the couplet "If they call me man-hater, you / would have known it for a lie," and the next couplet—"but the *you* I want to speak to / has become your death"—brings the sudden awareness that the "you" being addressed is Rich's husband, Alfred Conrad, who had died four years before. This poem becomes one instance of a colloquy with him that begins with "A Marriage in the Sixties" (1961) and resurfaces time and again through the ensuing decades in "From a Survivor" (1972), *Sources* (1981–1982), "Tattered Kaddish" (1989), the conclusion to section I of "An Atlas of the Difficult World," and "Shattered Head" (1996–1997). Rich's father is the direct addressee in "After Dark" (1964), "The Stelae" (1969), and sections of *Sources*; her mother in "Solfeggieto" (1985–1988). Michelle Cliff, an unspoken presence in any number of poems, is the "you" of the love celebrated in "Memorize This" (2002–2003) and is the person included in the pronoun "we" in "For an Anniversary" (1996).

In her perceptive review of Rich's *Collected Poems* published in *The American Scholar*, Sandra Gilbert noted two allusions to "invisible ink" that show the intertwining of personal and political in Rich's work. The first is in "Living Memory" (1988) and seems part of a general observation on the hidden lives of past Vermont settlers: "Written-across like nineteenth-century letters / or secrets penned in vinegar, invisible / till the page is held over flame." Yet that verse paragraph begins with an autobiographical statement: "I was left the legacy of a pile of stovewood / split by a man in the mute chains of rage." The next verse paragraph, immediately following mention of words "invisible / till the page is held over flame," again makes an autobiographical statement that begins with the same words: "I was left the legacy of three sons." The strong suggestion is that the poet, herself a sometime Vermont-dweller, uses the strategies of those nineteenth-century letter writers to inscribe herself into the records of her life in time.

The image resurfaces in the final section of "Endpapers" (2011), the last poem in Rich's last book, and stands there as an inscription on a grave monument, a "stele": it asserts the principles constant through all the changes in her life's work and asks her readers to look within that work for the timeless truth of its creator:

> The signature to a life requires
> the search for a method
> rejection of posturing
> trust in the witnesses
> a vial of invisible ink
> a sheet of paper held steady
> after the end-stroke
> above a deciphering flame

from

A CHANGE
OF WORLD

(1951)

STORM WARNINGS

The glass has been falling all the afternoon,
And knowing better than the instrument
What winds are walking overhead, what zone
Of gray unrest is moving across the land,
I leave the book upon a pillowed chair
And walk from window to closed window, watching
Boughs strain against the sky

And think again, as often when the air
Moves inward toward a silent core of waiting,
How with a single purpose time has traveled
By secret currents of the undiscerned
Into this polar realm. Weather abroad
And weather in the heart alike come on
Regardless of prediction.

Between foreseeing and averting change
Lies all the mastery of elements
Which clocks and weatherglasses cannot alter.
Time in the hand is not control of time,
Nor shattered fragments of an instrument
A proof against the wind; the wind will rise,
We can only close the shutters.

I draw the curtains as the sky goes black
And set a match to candles sheathed in glass
Against the keyhole draught, the insistent whine
Of weather through the unsealed aperture.
This is our sole defense against the season;
These are the things that we have learned to do
Who live in troubled regions.

AUNT JENNIFER'S TIGERS

Aunt Jennifer's tigers prance across a screen,
Bright topaz denizens of a world of green.
They do not fear the men beneath the tree;
They pace in sleek chivalric certainty.

Aunt Jennifer's fingers fluttering through her wool
Find even the ivory needle hard to pull.
The massive weight of Uncle's wedding band
Sits heavily upon Aunt Jennifer's hand.

When Aunt is dead, her terrified hands will lie
Still ringed with ordeals she was mastered by.
The tigers in the panel that she made
Will go on prancing, proud and unafraid.

AIR WITHOUT INCENSE

We eat this body and remain ourselves.
We drink this liquor, tasting wine, not blood.
Among these triple icons, rites of seven,
We know the feast to be of earth, not heaven:
Here man is wounded, yet we speak of God.
More than the Nazarene with him was laid
Into the tomb, and in the tomb has stayed.

Communion of no saints, mass without bell,
Air without incense, we implore at need.
There are questions to be answered, and the sky
Answers no questions, hears no litany.
We breathe the vapors of a sickened creed.

Ours are assassins deadlier than sin;
Deeper disorders starve the soul within.

If any writ could tell us, we would read.
If any ghost dared lay on us a claim,
Our fibers would respond, our nerves obey;
But revelation moves apart today
From gestures of a tired pontifical game.
We seek, where lamp and kyrie expire,
A site unscourged by wasting tongues of fire.

AFTERWARD

Now that your hopes are shamed, you stand
At last believing and resigned,
And none of us who touch your hand
Know how to give you back in kind
The words you flung when hopes were proud:
Being born to happiness
Above the asking of the crowd,
You would not take a finger less.
We who know limits now give room
To one who grows to fit her doom.

THE UNCLE SPEAKS IN THE
DRAWING ROOM

I have seen the mob of late
Standing sullen in the square,
Gazing with a sullen stare
At window, balcony, and gate.
Some have talked in bitter tones,
Some have held and fingered stones.

These are follies that subside.
Let us consider, none the less,
Certain frailties of glass
Which, it cannot be denied,
Lead in times like these to fear
For crystal vase and chandelier.

Not that missiles will be cast;
None as yet dare lift an arm.
But the scene recalls a storm
When our grandsire stood aghast
To see his antique ruby bowl
Shivered in a thunder-roll.

Let us only bear in mind
How these treasures handed down
From a calmer age passed on
Are in the keeping of our kind.
We stand between the dead glass-blowers
And murmurings of missile-throwers.

AN UNSAID WORD

She who has power to call her man
From that estranged intensity
Where his mind forages alone,
Yet keeps her peace and leaves him free,
And when his thoughts to her return
Stands where he left her, still his own,
Knows this the hardest thing to learn.

AT A BACH CONCERT

Coming by evening through the wintry city
We said that art is out of love with life.
Here we approach a love that is not pity.

This antique discipline, tenderly severe,
Renews belief in love yet masters feeling,
Asking of us a grace in what we bear.

Form is the ultimate gift that love can offer—
The vital union of necessity
With all that we desire, all that we suffer.

A too-compassionate art is half an art.
Only such proud restraining purity
Restores the else-betrayed, too-human heart.

THE SPRINGBOARD

Like divers, we ourselves must make the jump
That sets the taut board bounding underfoot
Clean as an axe blade driven in a stump;
But afterward what makes the body shoot
Into its pure and irresistible curve
Is of a force beyond all bodily powers.
So action takes velocity with a verve
Swifter, more sure than any will of ours.

FOR THE CONJUNCTION OF
TWO PLANETS

We smile at astrological hopes
And leave the sky to expert men
Who do not reckon horoscopes
But painfully extend their ken
In mathematical debate
With slide and photographic plate.

And yet, protest it if we will,
Some corner of the mind retains
The medieval man, who still
Keeps watch upon those starry skeins
And drives us out of doors at night
To gaze at anagrams of light.

Whatever register or law
Is drawn in digits for these two,
Venus and Jupiter keep their awe,
Wardens of brilliance, as they do

Their dual circuit of the west—
The brightest planet and her guest.

Is any light so proudly thrust
From darkness on our lifted faces
A sign of something we can trust,
Or is it that in starry places
We see the things we long to see
In fiery iconography?

from

THE
DIAMOND
CUTTERS

(1955)

LIVING IN SIN

She had thought the studio would keep itself;
no dust upon the furniture of love.
Half heresy, to wish the taps less vocal,
the panes relieved of grime. A plate of pears,
a piano with a Persian shawl, a cat
stalking the picturesque amusing mouse
had risen at his urging.
Not that at five each separate stair would writhe
under the milkman's tramp; that morning light
so coldly would delineate the scraps
of last night's cheese and three sepulchral bottles;
that on the kitchen shelf among the saucers
a pair of beetle-eyes would fix her own—
envoy from some village in the moldings . . .
Meanwhile, he, with a yawn,
sounded a dozen notes upon the keyboard,
declared it out of tune, shrugged at the mirror,
rubbed at his beard, went out for cigarettes;
while she, jeered by the minor demons,
pulled back the sheets and made the bed and found
a towel to dust the table-top,
and let the coffee-pot boil over on the stove.
By evening she was back in love again,
though not so wholly but throughout the night
she woke sometimes to feel the daylight coming
like a relentless milkman up the stairs.

THE SNOW QUEEN

Child with a chip of mirror in his eye
Saw the world ugly, fled to plains of ice
Where beauty was the Snow Queen's promises.
Under my lids a splinter sharp as his
Has made me wish you lying dead
Whose image digs the needle deeper still.

In the deceptive province of my birth
I had seen yes turn no, the saints descend,
Their sacred faces twisted into smiles,
The stars gone lechering, the village spring
Gush mud and toads—all miracles
Befitting an incalculable age.

To love a human face was to discover
The cracks of paint and varnish on the brow;
Soon to distrust all impulses of flesh
That strews its sawdust on the chamber floor,
While at the window peer two crones
Who once were Juliet and Jessica.

No matter, since I kept a little while
One thing intact from that perversity—
Though landscapes bloomed in monstrous cubes and coils.
In you belonged simplicities of light
To mend distraction, teach the air
To shine, the stars to find their way again.

Yet here the Snow Queen's cold prodigious will
Commands me, and your face has lost its power,
Dissolving to its opposite like the rest.
Under my ribs a diamond splinter now
Sticks, and has taken root; I know
Only this frozen spear that drives me through.

A WALK BY THE CHARLES

Finality broods upon the things that pass:
Persuaded by this air, the trump of doom
Might hang unsounded while the autumn gloom
Darkens the leaf and smokes the river's glass.
For nothing so susceptible to death
But on this forenoon seems to hold its breath:
The silent single oarsmen on the stream
Are always young, are rowers in a dream.
The lovers underneath the chestnut tree,
Though love is over, stand bemused to see
The season falling where no fall could be.

You oarsmen, when you row beyond the bend,
Will see the river winding to its end.
Lovers that hold the chestnut burr in hand
Will speak at last of death, will understand,
Foot-deep amid the ruinage of the year,
What smell it is that stings the gathering air.

From our evasion we are brought at last,
From all our hopes of constancy, to cast
One look of recognition at the sky,
The unimportant leaves that flutter by.
Why else upon this bank are we so still?
What lends us anchor but the mutable?

O lovers, let the bridge of your two hands
Be broken, like the mirrored bridge that bends
And shivers on the surface of the stream.
Young oarsmen, who in timeless gesture seem
Continuous, united with the tide,
Leave off your bending to the oar, and glide
Past innocence, beyond these aging bricks
To where the Charles flows in to join the Styx.

THE MIDDLE-AGED

Their faces, safe as an interior
Of Holland tiles and Oriental carpet,
Where the fruit-bowl, always filled, stood in a light
Of placid afternoon—their voices' measure,
Their figures moving in the Sunday garden
To lay the tea outdoors or trim the borders,
Afflicted, haunted us. For to be young
Was always to live in other people's houses
Whose peace, if we sought it, had been made by others,
Was ours at second-hand and not for long.
The custom of the house, not ours, the sun
Fading the silver-blue Fortuny curtains,
The reminiscence of a Christmas party
Of fourteen years ago—all memory,
Signs of possession and of being possessed,
We tasted, tense with envy. They were so kind,
Would have given us anything; the bowl of fruit
Was filled for us, there was a room upstairs
We must call ours: but twenty years of living
They could not give. Nor did they ever speak
Of the coarse stain on that polished balustrade,
The crack in the study window, or the letters
Locked in a drawer and the key destroyed.
All to be understood by us, returning
Late, in our own time—how that peace was made,
Upon what terms, with how much left unsaid.

THE DIAMOND CUTTERS

However legendary,
The stone is still a stone,
Though it had once resisted
The weight of Africa,
The hammer-blows of time
That wear to bits of rubble
The mountain and the pebble—
But not this coldest one.

Now, you intelligence
So late dredged up from dark
Upon whose smoky walls
Bison took fumbling form
Or flint was edged on flint—
Now, careful arriviste,
Delineate at will
Incisions in the ice.

Be serious, because
The stone may have contempt
For too-familiar hands,
And because all you do
Loses or gains by this:
Respect the adversary,
Meet it with tools refined,
And thereby set your price.

Be hard of heart, because
The stone must leave your hand.
Although you liberate
Pure and expensive fires
Fit to enamor Shebas,
Keep your desire apart.

Love only what you do,
And not what you have done.

Be proud, when you have set
The final spoke of flame
In that prismatic wheel,
And nothing's left this day
Except to see the sun
Shine on the false and the true,
And know that Africa
Will yield you more to do.

from

SNAPSHOTS
OF A
DAUGHTER-
IN-LAW

(1963)

THE KNIGHT

A knight rides into the noon,
and his helmet points to the sun,
and a thousand splintered suns
are the gaiety of his mail.
The soles of his feet glitter
and his palms flash in reply,
and under his crackling banner
he rides like a ship in sail.

A knight rides into the noon,
and only his eye is living,
a lump of bitter jelly
set in a metal mask,
betraying rags and tatters
that cling to the flesh beneath
and wear his nerves to ribbons
under the radiant casque.

Who will unhorse this rider
and free him from between
the walls of iron, the emblems
crushing his chest with their weight?
Will they defeat him gently,
or leave him hurled on the green,
his rags and wounds still hidden
under the great breastplate?

1957

SEPTEMBER 21

Wear the weight of equinoctial evening,
light like melons bruised on all the porches.
Feel the houses tenderly appraise you,
hold you in the watchfulness of mothers.

Once the nighttime was a milky river
washing past the swimmers in the sunset,
rinsing over sleepers of the morning.
Soon the night will be an eyeless quarry

where the shrunken daylight and its rebels,
loosened,   dive like stones in perfect silence,
names and voices drown without reflection.

Then the houses draw you. Then they have you.

1958

SNAPSHOTS OF A DAUGHTER-IN-LAW

1.

You, once a belle in Shreveport,
with henna-colored hair, skin like a peachbud,
still have your dresses copied from that time,
and play a Chopin prelude
called by Cortot: *"Delicious recollections*
float like perfume through the memory."

Your mind now, mouldering like wedding-cake,
heavy with useless experience, rich
with suspicion, rumor, fantasy,
crumbling to pieces under the knife-edge
of mere fact. In the prime of your life.

Nervy, glowering, your daughter
wipes the teaspoons, grows another way.

2.

Banging the coffee-pot into the sink
she hears the angels chiding, and looks out
past the raked gardens to the sloppy sky.
Only a week since They said: *Have no patience.*

The next time it was: *Be insatiable.*
Then: *Save yourself; others you cannot save.*
Sometimes she's let the tapstream scald her arm,
a match burn to her thumbnail,

or held her hand above the kettle's snout
right in the woolly steam. They are probably angels,
since nothing hurts her any more, except
each morning's grit blowing into her eyes.

3.

A thinking woman sleeps with monsters.
The beak that grips her, she becomes. And Nature,
that sprung-lidded, still commodious
steamer-trunk of *tempora* and *mores*
gets stuffed with it all: the mildewed orange-flowers,

the female pills, the terrible breasts
of Boadicea beneath flat foxes' heads and orchids.

Two handsome women, gripped in argument,
each proud, acute, subtle, I hear scream
across the cut glass and majolica
like Furies cornered from their prey:
The argument *ad feminam*, all the old knives
that have rusted in my back, I drive in yours,
ma semblable, ma soeur!

4.

Knowing themselves too well in one another:
their gifts no pure fruition, but a thorn,
the prick filed sharp against a hint of scorn . . .
Reading while waiting
for the iron to heat,
writing, *My Life had stood—a Loaded Gun—*
in that Amherst pantry while the jellies boil and scum,
or, more often,
iron-eyed and beaked and purposed as a bird,
dusting everything on the whatnot every day of life.

5.

Dulce ridens, dulce loquens,
she shaves her legs until they gleam
like petrified mammoth-tusk.

6.

When to her lute Corinna sings
neither words nor music are her own;
only the long hair dipping
over her cheek, only the song
of silk against her knees
and these
adjusted in reflections of an eye.

Poised, trembling and unsatisfied, before
an unlocked door, that cage of cages,
tell us, you bird, you tragical machine—
is this *fertilisante douleur?* Pinned down
by love, for you the only natural action,
are you edged more keen
to prise the secrets of the vault? has Nature shown
her household books to you, daughter-in-law,
that her sons never saw?

7.

"To have in this uncertain world some stay
which cannot be undermined, is
of the utmost consequence."
                              Thus wrote
a woman, partly brave and partly good,
who fought with what she partly understood.
Few men about her would or could do more,
hence she was labelled harpy, shrew and whore.

8.

"You all die at fifteen," said Diderot,
and turn part legend, part convention.
Still, eyes inaccurately dream
behind closed windows blankening with steam.
Deliciously, all that we might have been,
all that we were—fire, tears,
wit, taste, martyred ambition—
stirs like the memory of refused adultery
the drained and flagging bosom of our middle years.

9.

Not that it is done well, but
that it is done at all? Yes, think
of the odds! or shrug them off forever.
This luxury of the precocious child,
Time's precious chronic invalid,—
would we, darlings, resign it if we could?
Our blight has been our sinecure:
mere talent was enough for us—
glitter in fragments and rough drafts.

Sigh no more, ladies.
                        Time is male
and in his cups drinks to the fair.
Bemused by gallantry, we hear
our mediocrities over-praised,
indolence read as abnegation,
slattern thought styled intuition,
every lapse forgiven, our crime
only to cast too bold a shadow
or smash the mould straight off.

For that, solitary confinement,
tear gas, attrition shelling.
Few applicants for that honor.

10.

                           Well,
she's long about her coming, who must be
more merciless to herself than history.
Her mind full to the wind, I see her plunge
breasted and glancing through the currents,
taking the light upon her
at least as beautiful as any boy
or helicopter,
                poised, still coming,
her fine blades making the air wince
but her cargo
no promise then:
delivered
palpable
ours.

1958–1960

ANTINOÜS: THE DIARIES

Autumn torture. The old signs
smeared on the pavement, sopping leaves
rubbed into the landscape as unguent on a bruise,
brought indoors, even, as they bring flowers, enormous,
with the colors of the body's secret parts.

All this. And then, evenings, needing to be out,
walking fast, fighting the fire
that must die, light that sets my teeth on edge with joy,
till on the black embankment
I'm a cart stopped in the ruts of time.

Then at some house the rumor of truth and beauty
saturates a room like lilac-water
in the stream of a bath, fires snap, heads are high,
gold hair at napes of necks, gold in glasses,
gold in the throat, poetry of furs and manners.
Why do I shiver then? Haven't I seen,
over and over, before the end of an evening,
the three opened coffins carried in and left in a corner?
Haven't I watched as somebody cracked his shin
on one of them, winced and hopped and limped
laughing to lay his hand on a beautiful arm
striated with hairs of gold, like an almond-shell?

The old, needless story. For if I'm here
it is by choice and when at last
I smell my own rising nausea, feel the air
tighten around my stomach like a surgical bandage,
I can't pretend surprise. What is it I so miscarry?
If what I spew on the tiles at last,
helpless, disgraced, alone,
is in part what I've swallowed from glasses, eyes,
motions of hands, opening and closing mouths,
Isn't it also dead gobbets of myself,
abortive, murdered, or never willed?

1959

THE AFTERWAKE

Nursing your nerves
to rest, I've roused my own; well,
now for a few bad hours!
Sleep sees you behind closed doors.
Alone, I slump in his front parlor.
You're safe inside. Good. But I'm
like a midwife who at dawn
has all in order: bloodstains
washed up, teapot on the stove,
and starts her five miles home
walking, the birthyell still
exploding in her head.

Yes, I'm with her now: here's
the streaked, livid road
edged with shut houses
breathing night out and in.
Legs tight with fatigue,
we move under morning's coal-blue star,
colossal as this load
of unexpired purpose, which drains
slowly, till scissors of cockcrow snip the air.

1961

A MARRIAGE IN THE 'SIXTIES

As solid-seeming as antiquity,
you frown above
the *New York Sunday Times*

where Castro, like a walk-on out of *Carmen*,
mutters into a bearded henchman's ear.

They say the second's getting shorter—
I knew it in my bones—
and pieces of the universe are missing.
I feel the gears of this late afternoon
slip, cog by cog, even as I read.
"I'm old," we both complain,
half-laughing, oftener now.

Time serves you well. That face—
part Roman emperor, part Raimu—
nothing this side of Absence can undo.
Bliss, revulsion, your rare angers can
only carry through what's well begun.

When
I read your letters long ago
in that half-defunct
hotel in Magdalen Street
every word primed my nerves.
A geographical misery
composed of oceans, fogbound planes
and misdelivered cablegrams
lay round me, a Nova Zembla
only your live breath could unfreeze.
Today we stalk
in the raging desert of our thought
whose single drop of mercy is
each knows the other there.
Two strangers, thrust for life upon a rock,
may have at last the perfect hour of talk
that language aches for; still—
two minds, two messages.

Your brows knit into flourishes. Some piece
of mere time has you tangled there.
Some mote of history has flown into your eye.
Will nothing ever be the same,
even our quarrels take a different key,
our dreams exhume new metaphors?
The world breathes underneath our bed.
Don't look. We're at each other's mercy too.

Dear fellow-particle, electric dust
I'm blown with—ancestor
to what euphoric cluster—
see how particularity dissolves
in all that hints of chaos. Let one finger
hover toward you from There
and see this furious grain
suspend its dance to hang
beside you like your twin.

1961

GHOST OF A CHANCE

You see a man
trying to think.

You want to say
to everything:
Keep off! Give him room!
But you only watch,
terrified
the old consolations

will get him at last
like a fish
half-dead from flopping
and almost crawling
across the shingle,
almost breathing
the raw, agonizing
air
till a wave
pulls it back blind into the triumphant
sea.

1962

PROSPECTIVE
IMMIGRANTS
PLEASE NOTE

Either you will
go through this door
or you will not go through.

If you go through
there is always the risk
of remembering your name.

Things look at you doubly
and you must look back
and let them happen.

If you do not go through
it is possible
to live worthily

to maintain your attitudes
to hold your position
to die bravely

but much will blind you,
much will evade you,
at what cost who knows?

The door itself
makes no promises.
It is only a door.

1962

THE ROOFWALKER

For Denise Levertov

Over the half-finished houses
night comes. The builders
stand on the roof. It is
quiet after the hammers,
the pulleys hang slack.
Giants, the roofwalkers,
on a listing deck, the wave
of darkness about to break
on their heads. The sky
is a torn sail where figures
pass magnified, shadows
on a burning deck.

I feel like them up there:
exposed, larger than life,
and due to break my neck.

Was it worth while to lay—
with infinite exertion—
a roof I can't live under?
—All those blueprints,
closings of gaps,
measurings, calculations?
A life I didn't choose
chose me: even
my tools are the wrong ones
for what I have to do.
I'm naked, ignorant,
a naked man fleeing
across the roofs
who could with a shade of difference
be sitting in the lamplight
against the cream wallpaper
reading—not with indifference—
about a naked man
fleeing across the roofs.

1961

from

NECESSITIES
OF LIFE

(1966)

NECESSITIES OF LIFE

Piece by piece I seem
to re-enter the world: I first began

a small, fixed dot, still see
that old myself, a dark-blue thumbtack

pushed into the scene,
a hard little head protruding

from the pointillist's buzz and bloom.
After a time the dot

begins to ooze. Certain heats
melt it.
    Now I was hurriedly

blurring into ranges
of burnt red, burning green,

whole biographies swam up and
swallowed me like Jonah.

Jonah! I was Wittgenstein,
Mary Wollstonecraft, the soul

of Louis Jouvet, dead
in a blown-up photograph.

Till, wolfed almost to shreds,
I learned to make myself

unappetizing. Scaly as a dry bulb
thrown into a cellar

I used myself, let nothing use me.
Like being on a private dole,

sometimes more like kneading bricks in Egypt.
What life was there, was mine,

now and again to lay
one hand on a warm brick

and touch the sun's ghost
with economical joy,

now and again to name
over the bare necessities.

So much for those days. Soon
practice may make me middling-perfect, I'll

dare inhabit the world
trenchant in motion as an eel, solid

as a cabbage-head. I have invitations:
a curl of mist steams upward

from a field, visible as my breath,
houses along a road stand waiting

like old women knitting, breathless
to tell their tales.

1962

IN THE WOODS

"Difficult ordinary happiness,"
no one nowadays believes in you.
I shift, full-length on the blanket,
to fix the sun precisely

behind the pine-tree's crest
so light spreads through the needles
alive as water just
where a snake has surfaced,

unreal as water in green crystal.
Bad news is always arriving.
"We're hiders, hiding from something bad,"
sings the little boy.

Writing these words in the woods,
I feel like a traitor to my friends,
even to my enemies.
The common lot's to die

a stranger's death and lie
rouged in the coffin, in a dress
chosen by the funeral director.
Perhaps that's why we never

see clocks on public buildings any more.
A fact no architect will mention.
We're hiders, hiding from something bad
most of the time.

Yet, and outrageously, something good
finds us, found me this morning
lying on a dusty blanket
among the burnt-out Indian pipes

and bursting-open lady's-slippers.
My soul, my helicopter, whirred
distantly, by habit, over
the old pond with the half-drowned boat

toward which it always veers
for consolation: ego's Arcady:
leaving the body stuck
like a leaf against a screen.——

Happiness! how many times
I've stranded on that word,
at the edge of that pond; seen
as if through tears, the dragon-fly——

only to find it all
going differently for once
this time: my soul wheeled back
and burst into my body.

Found! ready or not.
If I move now, the sun
naked between the trees
will melt me as I lie.

1963

THE CORPSE-PLANT

How dare a sick man, or an obedient man, write poems?

—Whitman

A milk-glass bowl hanging by three chains
from the discolored ceiling
is beautiful tonight. On the floor, leaves, crayons,
innocent dust foregather.

Neither obedient nor sick, I turn my head,
feeling the weight of a thick gold ring
in either lobe. I see the corpse-plants
clustered in a hobnailed tumbler

at my elbow, white as death, I'd say,
if I'd ever seen death;
whiter than life
next to my summer-stained hand.

Is it in the sun that truth begins?
Lying under that battering light
the first few hours of summer
I felt scraped clean, washed down

to ignorance. The gold in my ears,
souvenir of a shrewd old city,
might have been wearing thin as wires
found in the bones of a woman's head

miraculously kept in its essentials
in some hot cradle-tomb of time.
I felt my body slipping through
the fingers of its mind.

Later, I slid on wet rocks,
threw my shoes across a brook,
waded on algae-furred stones
to join them. That day I found

the corpse-plants, growing like
shadows on a negative
in the chill of fern and lichen-rust.
That day for the first time

I gave them their deathly names—
or did they name themselves?—
not "Indian pipes" as once
we children knew them.

Tonight, I think of winter,
winters of mind, of flesh,
sickness of the rot-smell of leaves
turned silt-black, heavy as tarpaulin,

obedience of the elevator cage
lowering itself, crank by crank
into the mine-pit,
forced labor forcibly renewed—

but the horror is dimmed:
like the negative of one
intolerable photograph
it barely sorts itself out

under the radiance of the milk-glass shade.
Only death's insect whiteness
crooks its neck in a tumbler
where I placed its sign by choice.

1963

42

THE TREES

The trees inside are moving out into the forest,
the forest that was empty all these days
where no bird could sit
no insect hide
no sun bury its feet in shadow
the forest that was empty all these nights
will be full of trees by morning.

All night the roots work
to disengage themselves from the cracks
in the veranda floor.
The leaves strain toward the glass
small twigs stiff with exertion
long-cramped boughs shuffling under the roof
like newly discharged patients
half-dazed, moving
to the clinic doors.

I sit inside, doors open to the veranda
writing long letters
in which I scarcely mention the departure
of the forest from the house.
The night is fresh, the whole moon shines
in a sky still open
the smell of leaves and lichen
still reaches like a voice into the rooms.
My head is full of whispers
which tomorrow will be silent.

Listen. The glass is breaking.
The trees are stumbling forward
into the night. Winds rush to meet them.
The moon is broken like a mirror,

its pieces flash now in the crown
of the tallest oak.

1963

LIKE THIS TOGETHER
For A.H.C.

1.

Wind rocks the car.
We sit parked by the river,
silence between our teeth.
Birds scatter across islands
of broken ice. Another time
I'd have said "Canada geese,"
knowing you love them.
A year, ten years from now
I'll remember this—
this sitting like drugged birds
in a glass case—
not why, only that we
were here like this together.

2.

They're tearing down, tearing up
this city, block by block.
Rooms cut in half
hang like flayed carcasses,

their old roses in rags,
famous streets have forgotten
where they were going. Only
a fact could be so dreamlike.
They're tearing down the houses
we met and lived in,
soon our two bodies will be all
left standing from that era.

3.

We have, as they say,
certain things in common.
I mean: a view
from a bathroom window
over slate to stiff pigeons
huddled every morning; the way
water tastes from our tap,
which you marvel at, letting
it splash into the glass.
Because of you I notice
the taste of water,
a luxury I might
otherwise have missed.

4.

Our words misunderstand us.
Sometimes at night
you are my mother:
old detailed griefs
twitch at my dreams, and I
crawl against you, fighting

for shelter, making you
my cave. Sometimes
you're the wave of birth
that drowns me in my first
nightmare. I suck the air.
Miscarried knowledge twists us
like hot sheets thrown askew.

5.

Dead winter doesn't die,
it wears away, a piece of carrion
picked clean at last,
rained away or burnt dry.
Our desiring does this,
make no mistake, I'm speaking
of fact: through mere indifference
we could prevent it.
Only our fierce attention
gets hyacinths out of those
hard cerebral lumps,
unwraps the wet buds down
the whole length of a stem.

1963

AFTER DARK

I.

You are falling asleep and I sit looking at you
old tree of life
old man whose death I wanted
I can't stir you up now.

Faintly a phonograph needle
Whirs round in the last groove
eating my heart to dust.
That terrible record! how it played

down years, wherever I was
in foreign languages even
over and over, *I know you better
than you know yourself   I know*

*you better than you know
yourself   I know
you*   until, self-maimed,
I limped off, torn at the roots,

stopped singing a whole year,
got a new body, new breath,
got children, croaked for words,
forgot to listen

or read your *mene tekel* fading on the wall,
woke up one morning
and knew myself your daughter.
Blood is a sacred poison.

Now, unasked, you give ground.
We only want to stifle
what's stifling us already.
Alive now, root to crown, I'd give

—oh,—something—not to know
our struggles now are ended.
I seem to hold you, cupped
in my hands, and disappearing.

When your memory fails—
no more to scourge my inconsistencies—
the sashcords of the world fly loose.
A window crashes

suddenly down. I go to the woodbox
and take a stick of kindling
to prop the sash again.
I grow protective toward the world.

II.

Now let's away from prison—
Underground seizures!
I used to huddle in the grave
I'd dug for you and bite

my tongue for fear it would babble
—Darling—
I thought they'd find me there
someday, sitting upright, shrunken,

my hair like roots and in my lap
a mess of broken pottery—

wasted libation—
and you embalmed beside me.

No, let's away. Even now
there's a walk between doomed elms
(whose like we shall not see much longer)
and something—grass and water—

an old dream-photograph.
I'll sit with you there and tease you
for wisdom, if you like,
waiting till the blunt barge

bumps along the shore.
Poppies burn in the twilight
like smudge pots.
I think you hardly see me

but—this is the dream now—
your fears blow out,
off, over the water.
At the last, your hand feels steady.

1964

"I AM IN DANGER—SIR—"

"Half-cracked" to Higginson, living,
afterward famous in garbled versions,
your hoard of dazzling scraps a battlefield,
now your old snood

mothballed at Harvard
and you in your variorum monument
equivocal to the end—
who are you?

Gardening the day-lily,
wiping the wine-glass stems,
your thought pulsed on behind
a forehead battered paper-thin,

you, woman, masculine
in single-mindedness,
for whom the word was more
than a symptom—

a condition of being.
Till the air buzzing with spoiled language
sang in your ears
of Perjury

and in your half-cracked way you chose
silence for entertainment,
chose to have it out at last
on your own premises.

1964

NOT LIKE THAT

It's so pure in the cemetery.
The children love to play up here.
It's a little town, a game of blocks,
a village packed in a box,
a pre-war German toy.
The turf is a bedroom carpet:
heal-all, strawberry flower
and hillocks of moss.
To come and sit here forever,
a cup of tea on one's lap
and one's eyes closed lightly, lightly,
perfectly still
in a nineteenth-century sleep!
it seems so normal to die.

Nobody sleeps here, children.
The little beds of white wrought iron
and the tall, kind, faceless nurse
are somewhere else, in a hospital
or the dreams of prisoners of war.
The drawers of this trunk are empty,
not even a snapshot
curls in a corner.

In Pullmans of childhood we lay
enthralled behind dark-green curtains,
and a little lamp burned blue
all night, for us. The day
was a dream too, even the oatmeal
under its silver lid, dream-cereal
spooned out in forests of spruce
skirting the green-black gorges,
thick woods of sleep, half prickle,

half lakes of fern.
To stay here forever
is not like that, nor even
simply to lie quite still,
the warm trickle of dream
staining the thick quiet.
The drawers of this trunk are empty.
They are all out of sleep up here.

1965

THE KNOT

In the heart of the queen anne's lace, a knot of blood.
For years I never saw it,

years of metallic vision,
spears glancing off a bright eyeball,

suns off a Swiss lake.
A foaming meadow; the Milky Way;

and there, all along, the tiny dark-red spider
sitting in the whiteness of the bridal web,

waiting to plunge his crimson knifepoint
into the white apparencies.

Little wonder the eye, healing, sees
for a long time through a mist of blood.

1965

MOTH HOUR

Space mildews at our touch.
The leaves of the poplar, slowly moving—
aren't they moth-white, there in the moonbeams?
A million insects die every twilight,
no one even finds their corpses.
Death, slowly moving among the bleached clouds,
knows us better than we know ourselves.

I am gliding backward away from those who knew me
as the moon grows thinner and finally shuts its lantern.
I can be replaced a thousand times,
a box containing death.
When you put out your hand to touch me
you are already reaching toward an empty space.

1965

FOCUS
For Bert Dreyfus

Obscurity has its tale to tell.
Like the figure on the studio-bed in the corner,

out of range, smoking, watching and waiting.
Sun pours through the skylight onto the worktable

making of a jar of pencils, a typewriter keyboard
more than they were. Veridical light . . .

Earth budges. Now an empty coffee-cup,
a whetstone, a handkerchief, take on

their sacramental clarity, fixed by the wand
of light as the thinker thinks to fix them in the mind.

O secret in the core of the whetstone, in the five
pencils splayed out like fingers of a hand!

The mind's passion is all for singling out.
Obscurity has another tale to tell.

1965

FACE TO FACE

Never to be lonely like that—
the Early American figure on the beach
in black coat and knee-breeches
scanning the didactic storm in privacy,

never to hear the prairie wolves
in their lunar hilarity
circling one's little all, one's claim
to be Law and Prophets

for all that lawlessness,
never to whet the appetite
weeks early, for a face, a hand
longed-for and dreaded—

How people used to meet!
starved, intense, the old
Christmas gifts saved up till spring,
and the old plain words,

and each with his God-given secret,
spelled out through months of snow and silence,
burning under the bleached scalp; behind dry lips
a loaded gun.

1965

from

LEAFLETS

(1969)

ORION

Far back when I went zig-zagging
through tamarack pastures
you were my genius, you
my cast-iron Viking, my helmed
lion-heart king in prison.
Years later now you're young

my fierce half-brother, staring
down from that simplified west
your breast open, your belt dragged down
by an oldfashioned thing, a sword
the last bravado you won't give over
though it weighs you down as you stride

and the stars in it are dim
and maybe have stopped burning.
But you burn, and I know it;
as I throw back my head to take you in
an old transfusion happens again:
divine astronomy is nothing to it.

Indoors I bruise and blunder,
break faith, leave ill enough
alone, a dead child born in the dark.
Night cracks up over the chimney,
pieces of time, frozen geodes
come showering down in the grate.

A man reaches behind my eyes
and finds them empty
a woman's head turns away
from my head in the mirror
children are dying my death
and eating crumbs of my life.

Pity is not your forte.
Calmly you ache up there
pinned aloft in your crow's nest,
my speechless pirate!
You take it all for granted
and when I look you back

it's with a starlike eye
shooting its cold and egotistical spear
where it can do least damage.
Breathe deep! No hurt, no pardon
out here in the cold with you
you with your back to the wall.

1965

HOLDING OUT

The hunters' shack will do,
abandoned, untended, unmended
in its cul-de-sac of alders.
Inside, who knows what
hovel-keeping essentials—
a grey saucepan, a broom, a clock
stopped at last autumn's last hour—
all or any, what matter.

The point is, it's a shelter,
a place more in- than outside.
From that we could begin.
And the wind is surely rising,
snow is in the alders.
Maybe the stovepipe is sound,

maybe the smoke will do us in
at first—no matter.

Late afternoons the ice
squeaks underfoot like mica,
and when the sun drops red and moon-
faced back of the gun-colored firs,
the best intentions are none too good.
Then we have to make a go of it
in the smoke with the dark outside
and our love in our boots at first—
no matter.

1965

IN THE EVENING

Three hours chain-smoking words
and you move on. We stand in the porch,
two archaic figures: a woman and a man.

The old masters, the old sources,
haven't a clue what we're about,
shivering here in the half-dark 'sixties.

Our minds hover in a famous impasse
and cling together. Your hand
grips mine like a railing on an icy night.

The wall of the house is bleeding. Firethorn!
The moon, cracked every which-way,
pushes steadily on.

1966

5:30 A.M.

Birds and periodic blood.
Old recapitulations.
The fox, panting, fire-eyed,
gone to earth in my chest.
How beautiful we are,
he and I, with our auburn
pelts, our trails of blood,
our miracle escapes,
our whiplash panic flogging us on
to new miracles!
They've supplied us with pills
for bleeding, pills for panic.
Wash them down the sink.
This is truth, then:
dull needle groping in the spinal fluid,
weak acid in the bottom of the cup,
foreboding, foreboding.
No one tells the truth about truth,
that it's what the fox
sees from his scuffled burrow:
dull-jawed, onrushing
killer, being that
inanely single-minded
will have our skins at last.

1967

THE KEY

Through a drain grating, something
    glitters and falters,
        glitters again. A scrap of foil,

a coin, a signal, a message
    from the indistinct
        piercing my indistinctness?

How long I have gone round
    and round, spiritless with foreknown defeat,
        in search of that glitter?

Hours, years maybe. The cry of metal
    on asphalt, on iron, the sudden
        ching of a precious loss,

the clear statement
    of something missing. Over and over
        it stops me in my tracks

like a falling star, only
    this is not the universe's loss
        it is mine. If I were only colder,

nearer death, nearer birth, I might let go
    whatever's so bent on staying lost.
        Why not leave the house

locked, to collapse inward among its weeds,
    the letters to darken and flake
        in the drawer, the car

to grow skeletal, aflame with rust
     in the moonlit lot, and walk
         ever after?

O God I am not spiritless,
     but a spirit can be stunned,
         a battery felt going dead

before the light flickers,
     and I've covered this ground too often
         with this yellow disc

within whose beam all's commonplace
     and whose limits are described
         by the whole night.

1967

ABNEGATION

The red fox, the vixen
dancing in the half-light among the junipers,
wise-looking in a sexy way,
Egyptian-supple in her sharpness—
what does she want
with the dreams of dead vixens,
the apotheosis of Reynard,
the literature of fox-hunting?
Only in her nerves the past
sings, a thrill of self-preservation.
I go along down the road
to a house nailed together by Scottish

Covenanters, instinct mortified
in a virgin forest,
and she springs toward her den
every hair on her pelt alive
with tidings of the immaculate present.
They left me a westernness,
a birthright, a redstained, ravelled
afghan of sky.
She has no archives,
no heirlooms, no future
except death
and I could be more
her sister than theirs
who chopped their way across these hills
—a chosen people.

1968

TO FRANTZ FANON
Born Martinique, 1925; dead Washington D.C., 1961.

I don't see your head
sunk, listening   to the throats
of the torturers and the tortured

I don't see your eyes
deep in the blackness   of your skull
they look off from me   into the eyes

of rats and haunted policemen.
What I see best is the length
of your fingers

pressing the pencil
into the barred page

of the French child's copybook
with its Cartesian squares   its grilled
trap of holy geometry
where your night-sweats streamed out
in language

and your death
a black streak on a white bed
in L'Enfant's city where
the fever-bush sweats off

its thick
petals   year after year
on the mass grave
of revolt

1968

ON EDGES

When the ice starts to shiver
all across the reflecting basin
or water-lily leaves
dissect a simple surface
the word 'drowning' flows through me.
You built a glassy floor
that held me
as I leaned to fish for old
hooks and toothed tin cans,

stems lashing out like ties of
silk dressing-gowns
archangels of lake-light
gripped in mud.

Now you hand me a torn letter.
On my knees, in the ashes, I could never
fit these ripped-up flakes together.
In the taxi I am still piecing
what syllables I can
translating at top speed like a thinking machine
that types out 'useless' as 'monster'
and 'history' as 'lampshade'.
Crossing the bridge I need all my nerve
to trust to the man-made cables.

The blades on that machine
could cut you to ribbons
but its function is humane.
Is this all I can say of these
delicate hooks, scythe-curved intentions
you and I handle? I'd rather
taste blood, yours or mine, flowing
from a sudden slash, than cut all day
with blunt scissors on dotted lines
like the teacher told.

1968

NIGHTBREAK

Something broken   Something
I need   By someone
I love   Next year
will I remember what
This anger   unreal
                              yet
has to be gone through
The sun to set
on this anger
                    I go on
head down   into it
The mountain pulsing
Into the oildrum   drops
the ball of fire.

Time is quiet   doesn't break things
or even wound   Things are in danger
from people   The frail clay lamps
of Mesopotamia
row on row under glass
in the ethnological section
little hollows for dried-
up oil   The refugees
with their identical
tales of escape   I don't
collect what I can't use   I need
what can be broken.

In the bed the pieces fly together
and the rifts fill   or else
my body is a list   of wounds
symmetrically placed
a village

blown open   by planes
that did not   finish the job

The enemy has   withdrawn
between raids   become invisible
there are
         no agencies
               of relief
the darkness becomes utter
Sleep   cracked and flaking
sifts over the shaken   target.

What breaks   is night
not day   The white
scar   splitting
over the east
The crack weeping
Time for the pieces
            to move
dumbly back
         toward each other.

1968

LEAFLETS

1.

The big star, and that other
lonely on black glass
overgrown with frozen
lesions, endless night
the Coal Sack gaping
black veins of ice on the pane
spelling a word:
               Insomnia
not manic but ordinary
to start out of sleep
turning off and on
this seasick neon
vision, this
division

the head clears of sweet smoke
and poison gas

life without caution
the only worth living
love for a man
love for a woman
love for the facts
protectless

that self-defense be not
the arm's first motion

memory not only
cards of identity

that I can live half a year
as I have never lived up to this time—

Chekhov coughing up blood almost daily
the steamer edging in toward the penal colony
chained men dozing on deck
five forest fires lighting the island

lifelong that glare, waiting.

2.

Your face
                    stretched like a mask
                                        begins to tear
as you speak of Che Guevara
Bolivia, Nanterre
I'm too young to be your mother
you're too young to be my brother

your tears are not political
they are real water, burning
as the tears of Telemachus
burned

Over Spanish Harlem the moon
swells up, a fire balloon
fire gnawing the edge
of this crushed-up newspaper

                                        now
the bodies come whirling
coal-black, ash-white
out of torn windows
and the death columns blacken

                    whispering
Who'd choose this life?

We're fighting for a slash of recognition,
a piercing to the pierced heart.
Tell me what you are going through—

but the attention flickers
                    and will flicker
a matchflame in poison air
a thread, a hair of light
                    sum of all answer
to the *Know that I exist!* of all existing things.

3.

If, says the Dahomeyan devil,
someone has courage to enter the fire
the young man will be restored to life.

If, the girl whispers,
I do not go into the fire
I will not be able to live with my soul.

(Her face calm and dark as amber
under the dyed butterfly turban
her back scarified in ostrich-skin patterns.)

4.

Crusaders' wind glinting
off linked scales of sea
ripping the ghostflags

galloping at the fortress
Acre, bloodcaked, lionhearted
raw vomit curdling in the sun
gray walkers walking
straying with a curbed intentness
in and out the inclosures
the gallows, the photographs
of dead Jewish terrorists, aged 15
their fading faces wide-eyed
and out in the crusading sunlight
gray strayers still straying
dusty paths
the mad who live in the dried-up moat
of the War Museum

what are we coming to
what wants these things of us
who wants them

5.

The strain of being born
        over and over has torn your smile into pieces
often I have seen it broken
        and then re-membered
and wondered how a beauty
        so anarch, so ungelded
will be cared for in this world.
        I want to hand you this
leaflet streaming with rain or tears
        but the words coming clear
something you might find crushed into your hand
        after passing a barricade
and stuff in your raincoat pocket.

I want this to reach you
who told me once that poetry is nothing sacred
        no more sacred that is
than other things in your life—
        to answer yes, if life is uncorrupted
no better poetry is wanted.
        I want this to be yours
in the sense that if you find and read it
        it will be there in you already
and the leaflet then merely something
        to leave behind, a little leaf
in the drawer of a sublet room.
        What else does it come down to
but handing on scraps of paper
        little figurines or phials
no stronger than the dry clay they are baked in
        yet more than dry clay or paper
because the imagination crouches in them.
        If we needed fire to remind us
that all true images
        were scooped out of the mud
where our bodies curse and flounder
        then perhaps that fire is coming
to sponge away the scribes and time-servers
        and much that you would have loved will be lost as well
before you could handle it and know it
        just as we almost miss each other
in the ill cloud of mistrust, who might have touched
        hands quickly, shared food or given blood
for each other. I am thinking how we can use what we have
        to invent what we need.

Winter—Spring 1968

from GHAZALS
(HOMAGE TO GHALIB)

7/13/68
The ones who camped on the slopes, below the bare summit,
saw differently from us, who breathed thin air and kept walking.

Sleeping back-to-back, man and woman, we were more conscious
than either of us awake and alone in the world.

These words are vapor-trails of a plane that has vanished;
by the time I write them out, they are whispering something else.

Do we still have to feel jealous of our creations?
Once they might have outlived us; in this world, we'll die together.

Don't look for me in the room I have left;
the photograph shows just a white rocking-chair, still rocking.

7/14/68: II

Did you think I was talking about my life?
I was trying to drive a tradition up against the wall.

The field they burned over is greener than all the rest.
You have to watch it, he said, the sparks can travel the roots.

Shot back into this earth's atmosphere
our children's children may photograph these stones.

In the red wash of the darkroom, I see myself clearly;
when the print is developed and handed about, the face is
        nothing to me.

For us the work undoes itself over and over:
the grass grows back, the dust collects, the scar breaks open.

7/24/68: II

The friend I can trust is the one who will let me have my death.
The rest are actors who want me to stay and further the plot.

At the drive-in movie, above the PanaVision,
beyond the projector beams, you project yourself, great Star.

The eye that used to watch us is dead, but open.
Sometimes I still have a sense of being followed.

How long will we be waiting for the police?
How long must I wonder which of my friends would hide me?

Driving at night I feel the Milky Way
streaming above me like the graph of a cry.

7/26/68: I

Last night you wrote on the wall: Revolution is poetry.
Today you needn't write; the wall has tumbled down.

We were taught to respect the appearance behind the reality.
Our senses were out on parole, under surveillance.

A pair of eyes imprisoned for years inside my skull
is burning its way outward, the headaches are terrible.

I'm walking through a rubble of broken sculpture, stumbling
here on the spine of a friend, there on the hand of a brother.

All those joinings! and yet we fought so hard to be unique.
Neither alone, nor in anyone's arms, will we end up sleeping.

8/8/68: II
For A.H.C.

A piece of thread ripped-out from a fierce design,
some weaving figured as magic against oppression.

I'm speaking to you as a woman to a man:
when your blood flows I want to hold you in my arms.

How did we get caught up fighting this forest fire,
we, who were only looking for a still place in the woods?

How frail we are, and yet, dispersed, always returning,
the barnacles they keep scraping from the warship's hull.

The hairs on your breast curl so lightly as you lie there,
while the strong heart goes on pounding in its sleep.

from

THE WILL
TO CHANGE

(1971)

What does not change / is the will to change

—Charles Olson, "The Kingfishers"

PLANETARIUM

*Thinking of Caroline Herschel, 1750–1848, astronomer,
sister of William; and others.*

A woman in the shape of a monster
a monster in the shape of a woman
the skies are full of them

a woman   'in the snow
among the Clocks and instruments
or measuring the ground with poles'

in her 98 years to discover
8 comets

she whom the moon ruled
like us
levitating into the night sky
riding the polished lenses

Galaxies of women, there
doing penance for impetuousness
ribs chilled
in those spaces   of the mind

An eye,
            'virile, precise and absolutely certain'
            from the mad webs of Uranusborg

                                    encountering the NOVA

every impulse of light exploding
from the core
as life flies out of us

        Tycho whispering at last
        'Let me not seem to have lived in vain'

What we see, we see
and seeing is changing

the light that shrivels a mountain
and leaves a man alive

Heartbeat of the pulsar
heart sweating through my body

The radio impulse
pouring in from Taurus

        I am bombarded yet   I stand

I have been standing all my life in the
direct path of a battery of signals
the most accurately transmitted most
untranslateable language in the universe
I am a galactic cloud so deep   so invo-
luted that a light wave could take 15
years to travel through me   And has
taken   I am an instrument in the shape
of a woman trying to translate pulsations
into images   for the relief of the body
and the reconstruction of the mind.

1968

THE BURNING OF PAPER INSTEAD OF CHILDREN

I was in danger of verbalizing my moral impulses out of existence.

—Fr. Daniel Berrigan, on trial in Baltimore

1.

My neighbor, a scientist and art-collector, telephones me in a state
of violent emotion. He tells me that my son and his, aged eleven
and twelve, have on the last day of school burned a mathematics
text-book in the backyard. He has forbidden my son to come to his
house for a week, and has forbidden his own son to leave the house
during that time. "The burning of a book," he says, "arouses terrible
sensations in me, memories of Hitler; there are few things that upset
me so much as the idea of burning a book."

Back there: the library, walled
with green Britannicas
Looking again
in Dürer's *Complete Works*
for MELENCOLIA, the baffled woman

the crocodiles in Herodotus
the Book of the Dead
the *Trial of Jeanne d'Arc,* so blue
I think, It is her color

and they take the book away
because I dream of her too often

love and fear in a house
knowledge of the oppressor

I know it hurts to burn

2.

To imagine a time of silence
or few words
a time of chemistry and music

the hollows above your buttocks
traced by my hand
or, *hair is like flesh,* you said

an age of long silence

relief

from this tongue   the slab of limestone
or reinforced concrete
fanatics and traders
dumped on this coast   wildgreen   clayred
that breathed once
in signals of smoke
sweep of the wind

knowledge of the oppressor
this is the oppressor's language

yet I need it to talk to you

3.

"People suffer highly in poverty and it takes dignity and intelligence
to overcome this suffering. Some of the suffering are: a child did not
had dinner last night: a child steal because he did not have money
to buy it: to hear a mother say she do not have money to buy food
for her children and to see a child without cloth it will make tears
in your eyes."

(the fracture of order
the repair of speech
to overcome this suffering)

4.

We lie under the sheet
after making love, speaking
of loneliness
relieved in a book
relived in a book
so on that page
the clot and fissure
of it appears
words of a man
in pain
a naked word
entering the clot
a hand grasping
through bars:

deliverance

What happens between us
has happened for centuries
we know it from literature

still it happens

sexual jealousy
outflung hand
beating bed

dryness of mouth
after panting

there are books that describe all this
and they are useless

You walk into the woods behind a house
there in that country
you find a temple
built eighteen hundred years ago
you enter without knowing
what it is you enter

so it is with us

no one knows what may happen
though the books tell everything

burn the texts   said Artaud

5.

I am composing on the typewriter late at night, thinking of today.
How well we all spoke. A language is a map of our failures. Fred-
erick Douglass wrote an English purer than Milton's. People suffer
highly in poverty. There are methods but we do not use them. Joan,
who could not read, spoke some peasant form of French. Some of
the suffering are: it is hard to tell the truth; this is America; I cannot
touch you now. In America we have only the present tense. I am in dan-
ger. You are in danger. The burning of a book arouses no sensation in
me. I know it hurts to burn. There are flames of napalm
in Catonsville, Maryland. I know it hurts to burn. The typewriter
is overheated, my mouth is burning, I cannot touch you and this is
the oppressor's language.

1968

I DREAM I'M THE
DEATH OF ORPHEUS

I am walking rapidly through striations of light and dark thrown
    under an arcade.

I am a woman in the prime of life, with certain powers
and those powers severely limited
by authorities whose faces I rarely see.
I am a woman in the prime of life
driving her dead poet in a black Rolls-Royce
through a landscape of twilight and thorns.
A woman with a certain mission
which if obeyed to the letter will leave her intact.
A woman with the nerves of a panther
a woman with contacts among Hell's Angels
a woman feeling the fullness of her powers
at the precise moment when she must not use them
a woman sworn to lucidity
who sees through the mayhem, the smoky fires
of these underground streets
her dead poet learning to walk backward against the wind
on the wrong side of the mirror

1968

THE BLUE GHAZALS

9/21/68

Violently asleep in the old house.
A clock stays awake all night ticking.

Turning, turning their bruised leaves
the trees stay awake all night in the wood.

Talk to me with your body through my dreams.
Tell me what we are going through.

The walls of the room are muttering,
old trees, old utopians, arguing with the wind.

To float like a dead man in a sea of dreams
and half those dreams being dreamed by someone else.

Fifteen years of sleepwalking with you,
wading against the tide, and with the tide.

9/23/68

One day of equinoctial light after another,
moving ourselves through gauzes and fissures of that light.

Early and late I come and set myself against you,
your phallic fist knocking blindly at my door.

The dew is beaded like mercury on the coarsened grass,
the web of the spider is heavy as if with sweat.

Everything is yielding toward a foregone conclusion,
only we are rash enough to go on changing our lives.

An Ashanti woman tilts the flattened basin on her head
to let the water slide downward: I am that woman and that water.

9/28/68: I

A man, a woman, a city.
The city as object of love.

Anger and filth in the basement.
The furnace stoked and blazing.

A sexual heat on the pavements.
Trees erected like statues.

Eyes at the ends of avenues.
Yellow for hesitation.

I'm tired of walking your streets
he says, unable to leave her.

Air of dust and rising sparks,
the city burning her letters.

9/28/68: II
For Wallace Stevens

Ideas of order . . . Sinner of the Florida keys,
you were our poet of revolution all along.

A man isn't what he seems but what he desires:
gaieties of anarchy drumming at the base of the skull.

Would this have left you cold, our scene, its wild parades,
the costumes, banners, incense, flowers, the immense marches?

Disorder is natural, these leaves absently blowing
in the drinking-fountain, filling the statue's crevice.

The use of force in public architecture:
nothing, not even the honeycomb, manifests such control.

9/29/68
For Leroi Jones

Late at night I went walking through your difficult wood,
half-sleepy, half-alert in that thicket of bitter roots.

Who doesn't speak to me, who speaks to me more and more,
but from a face turned off, turned away, a light shut out.

Most of the old lecturers are inaudible or dead.
Prince of the night there are explosions in the hall.

The blackboard scribbled over with dead languages
is falling and killing our children.

Terribly far away I saw your mouth in the wild light:
it seemed to me you were shouting instructions to us all.

12/13/68

They say, if you can tell, clasped tight under the blanket,
the edge of dark from the edge of dawn, your love is a lie.

If I thought of my words as changing minds,
hadn't my mind also to suffer changes?

They measure fever, swab the blisters of the throat,
but the cells of thought go rioting on ignored.

It's the inner ghost that suffers, little spirit
looking out wildly from the clouded pupils.

When will we lie clearheaded in our flesh again
with the cold edge of the night driving us close together?

12/20/68: I

There are days when I seem to have nothing
but these frayed packets, done up with rotting thread.

The shortest day of the year, let it be ours.
Let me give you something: a token for the subway.

(Refuse even
the most beloved old solutions.

That dead man wrote, grief ought to reach the lips.
You must believe I know before you can tell me.

A black run through the tunnelled winter, he and she,
together, touching, yet not side by side.

12/20/68: II

Frost, burning. The city's ill.
We gather like viruses.

The doctors are all on their yachts
watching the beautiful skin-divers.

The peasant mind of the Christian
transfixed on food at the year's turning.

Thinking of marzipan
forget that revolutionary child.

Thought grown senile with sweetness.
You too may visit the Virgins.

In the clear air, hijacked planes
touch down at the forbidden island.

5/4/69

Pain made her conservative.
Where the matches touched her flesh, she wears a scar.

The police arrive at dawn
like death and childbirth.

City of accidents, your true map
is the tangling of all our lifelines.

The moment when a feeling enters the body
is political. This touch is political.

Sometimes I dream we are floating on water
hand-in-hand; and sinking without terror.

OUR WHOLE LIFE

Our whole life a translation
the permissible fibs .

and now a knot of lies
eating at itself to get undone

Words bitten thru words

meanings burnt-off like paint
under the blowtorch

All those dead letters
rendered into the oppressor's language

Trying to tell the doctor where it hurts
like the Algerian
who has walked from his village, burning

his whole body a cloud of pain
and there are no words for this

except himself

1969

THE STELAE

For Arnold Rich

Last night I met you in my sister's house
risen from the dead
showing me your collection

You are almost at the point of giving things away

It's the stelae on the walls I want
that I never saw before

You offer other objects
I have seen time and time again

I think you think you are giving me
something precious

The stelae are so unlike you
swart, indifferent, incised with signs
you have never deciphered

I never knew you had them
I wonder if you are giving them away

1969

THE WILL TO CHANGE

1.

For L D., Dead 11/69

That Chinese restaurant was a joke
with its repeating fountains

& chopsticks in tissue paper
The vodka was too sweet

the beancurd too hot
You came with your Egyptian hieroglyph

your angel's smile
Almost the next day

as surely as if shot
you were thin air

At the risk of appearing ridiculous—
we take back this halfworld for you

and all whose murders accrue
past your death

2.

For Sandra Levinson

Knocked down in the canefield
by a clumsily swung machete

she is helped to her feet
by Fidel

and snapped by photographers
the blonde Yanqui in jeans

We're living through a time
that needs to be lived through us

(and in the morning papers
Bobby Seale, chalked

by the courtroom artist
defaced by the gag)

3.
For D.J.L.

Beardless again, phoning
from a storefront in Yorkville

. . . we need a typewriter, a crib
& Michael's number . . .

I swim to you thru dead
latitudes of fever

. . . accepting the discipline . . .
You mean your old freedom

to disappear—you miss that?
. . . but I can dig having lost it . . .

David, I could dig losing everything.
Knowing what you mean, to make that leap

bite into the fear, over & over
& survive. Hoarding my 'liberty'

like a compulsive—more
than I can use up in a lifetime—

two dozen oranges in the refrigerator
for one American weekend

4.
For A.H.C.

At the wings of the mirror, peacock plumes
from the Feast of San Gennaro

gaze thru the dark
All night the A-train forages

under our bedroom
All night I dream of a man

black, gagged, shackled, coffined
in a courtroom where I am

passive, white & silent
though my mouth is free

All night I see his eyes
iridescent under torture

and hear the shuddering of the earth
as the trains tear us apart

5.

The cabdriver from the Bronx
screaming: 'This city's GOTTA die!'

dynamiting it hourly from his soul
as surely as any terrorist

Burning the bodies of the scum on welfare
ejaculating into the flames

(*and*, said Freud,
who welcomed it when it was done?)

the professors of the fact
that someone has suffered

seeking truth in a mist of librium
the artists talking of freedom

in their chains

1969–1970

IMAGES FOR GODARD

1.

Language as city:: Wittgenstein
Driving to the limits
of the city of words

the superhighway streams
like a comic strip

to newer suburbs
casements of shockproof glass

where no one yet looks out
or toward the coast where even now

the squatters in their shacks
await eviction

When all conversation
becomes an interview
under duress

when we come to the limits
of the city

my face must have a meaning

2.

To know the extremes of light
I sit in this darkness

To see the present flashing
in a rearview mirror

blued in a plateglass pane
reddened in the reflection

of the red Triomphe
parked at the edge of the sea

the sea glittering in the sun
the swirls of nebula

in the espresso cup
raindrops, neon spectra

on a vinyl raincoat

3.

To love, to move perpetually
as the body changes

a dozen times a day
the temperature of the skin

the feeling of rise & fall
deadweight & buoyancy

the eye sunk inward
the eye bleeding with speech

('for that moment at least
I wás you—')

To be stopped, to shoot the same scene
over & over

4.

At the end of *Alphaville*
she says *I love you*

and the film begins
that you've said you'd never make

because it's impossible
'things as difficult to show

as horror & war & sickness are'

meaning: love,
to speak in the mouth

to touch the breast
for a woman

to know the sex of a man
That film begins here

yet you don't show it
we leave the theatre

suffering from that

5.

Interior monologue of the poet:
the notes for the poem are the only poem

the mind collecting, devouring
all these destructibles

the unmade studio couch the air
shifting the abalone shells

the mind of the poet is the only poem
the poet is at the movies

dreaming the film-maker's dream but differently
free in the dark as if asleep

free in the dusty beam of the projector
the mind of the poet is changing

the moment of change is the only poem

1970

A VALEDICTION
FORBIDDING MOURNING

My swirling wants. Your frozen lips.
The grammar turned and attacked me.
Themes, written under duress.
Emptiness of the notations.

They gave me a drug that slowed the healing of wounds.

I want you to see this before I leave:
the experience of repetition as death
the failure of criticism to locate the pain
the poster in the bus that said:
my bleeding is under control.

A red plant in a cemetery of plastic wreaths.

A last attempt: the language is a dialect called metaphor.
These images go unglossed: hair, glacier, flashlight.
When I think of a landscape I am thinking of a time.

When I talk of taking a trip I mean forever.
I could say: those mountains have a meaning
but further than that I could not say.

To do something very common, in my own way.

1970

from SHOOTING SCRIPT
PART I: 11/69–2/70

1.

We were bound on the wheel of an endless conversation.

Inside this shell, a tide waiting for someone to enter.

A monologue waiting for you to interrupt it.

A man wading into the surf. The dialogue of the rock with the breaker.

The wave changed instantly by the rock; the rock changed by the wave
returning over and over.

The dialogue that lasts all night or a whole lifetime.

A conversation of sounds melting constantly into rhythms.

A shell waiting for you to listen.

A tide that ebbs and flows against a deserted continent.

A cycle whose rhythm begins to change the meanings of words.

A wheel of blinding waves of light, the spokes pulsing out from where
we hang together in the turning of an endless conversation.

The meaning that searches for its word like a hermit crab.

A monologue that waits for one listener.

An ear filled with one sound only.

A shell penetrated by meaning.

PART II: 3–7/70

8.

For Hugh Seidman

A woman waking behind grimed blinds slatted across a courtyard
she never looks into.

Thinking of the force of a waterfall, the slash of cold air from the
thickest water of the falls, slicing the green and ochre afternoon in
which he turns his head and walks away.

Thinking of that place as an existence.

A woman reaching for the glass of water left all night on the bureau,
the half-done poem, the immediate relief.

Entering the poem as a method of leaving the room.

Entering the paper airplane of the poem, which somewhere before
its destination starts curling into ash and comes apart.

The woman is too heavy for the poem, she is a swollenness, a foot,
an arm, gone asleep, grown absurd and out of bounds.

Rooted to memory like a wedge in a block of wood; she takes the pressure of her thought but cannot resist it.

You call this a poetry of false problems, the shotgun wedding of the mind, the subversion of choice by language.

Instead of the alternative: to pull the sooty strings to set the window bare to purge the room with light to feel the sun breaking in on the courtyard and the steamheat smothering in the shut-off pipes.

To feel existence as this time, this place, the pathos and force of the lumps of snow gritted and melting in the unloved corners of the courtyard.

13.

We are driven to odd attempts; once it would not have occurred to me to put out in a boat, not on a night like this.

Still, it was an instrument, and I had pledged myself to try any instrument that came my way. Never to refuse one from conviction of incompetence.

A long time I was simply learning to handle the skiff; I had no special training and my own training was against me.

I had always heard that darkness and water were a threat.

In spite of this, darkness and water helped me to arrive here.

I watched the lights on the shore I had left for a long time; each one, it seemed to me, was a light I might have lit, in the old days.

14.

Whatever it was: the grains of the glacier caked in the boot-cleats;
ashes spilled on white formica.

The death-col viewed through power-glasses; the cube of ice
melting on stainless steel.

Whatever it was, the image that stopped you, the one on which you
came to grief, projecting it over & over on empty walls.

Now to give up the temptations of the projector; to see instead the
web of cracks filtering across the plaster.

To read there the map of the future, the roads radiating from the
initial split, the filaments thrown out from that impasse.

To reread the instructions on your palm; to find there how the
lifeline, broken, keeps its direction.

To read the etched rays of the bullet-hole left years ago in the
glass; to know in every distortion of the light what fracture is.

To put the prism in your pocket, the thin glass lens, the map
of the inner city, the little book with gridded pages.

To pull yourself up by your own roots; to eat the last meal in your old
neighborhood.

from

DIVING INTO
THE WRECK

(1973)

TRYING TO TALK WITH A MAN

Out in this desert we are testing bombs,

that's why we came here.

Sometimes I feel an underground river
forcing its way between deformed cliffs
an acute angle of understanding
moving itself like a locus of the sun
into this condemned scenery.

What we've had to give up to get here—
whole LP collections, films we starred in
playing in the neighborhoods, bakery windows
full of dry, chocolate-filled Jewish cookies,
the language of love-letters, of suicide notes,
afternoons on the riverbank
pretending to be children

Coming out to this desert
we meant to change the face of
driving among dull green succulents
walking at noon in the ghost town
surrounded by a silence

that sounds like the silence of the place
except that it came with us
and is familiar
and everything we were saying until now
was an effort to blot it out—
Coming out here we are up against it

Out here I feel more helpless
with you than without you

You mention the danger
and list the equipment
we talk of people caring for each other
in emergencies—laceration, thirst—
but you look at me like an emergency

Your dry heat feels like power
your eyes are stars of a different magnitude
they reflect lights that spell out: EXIT
when you get up and pace the floor

talking of the danger
as if it were not ourselves
as if we were testing anything else.

1971

WHEN WE DEAD AWAKEN
For E.Y.

1. Trying to tell you how
    the anatomy of the park
    through stained panes, the way
    guerrillas are advancing
    through minefields, the trash
    burning endlessly in the dump
    to return to heaven like a stain—
    everything outside our skins is an image
    of this affliction:
    stones on my table, carried by hand
    from scenes I trusted
    souvenirs of what I once described

as happiness
everything outside my skin
speaks of the fault that sends me limping
even the scars of my decisions
even the sunblaze in the mica-vein
even you, fellow-creature, sister,
sitting across from me, dark with love,
working like me to pick apart
working with me to remake
this trailing knitted thing, this cloth of darkness,
this woman's garment, trying to save the skein.

2.   The fact of being separate
enters your livelihood like a piece of furniture
—a chest of seventeenth-century wood
from somewhere in the North.
It has a huge lock shaped like a woman's head
but the key has not been found.
In the compartments are other keys
to lost doors, an eye of glass.
Slowly you begin to add
things of your own.
You come and go reflected in its panels.
You give up keeping track of anniversaries,
you begin to write in your diaries
more honestly than ever.

3.   The lovely landscape of southern Ohio
betrayed by strip mining, the
thick gold band on the adulterer's finger
the blurred programs of the offshore pirate station
are causes for hesitation.
Here in the matrix of need and anger, the
disproof of what we thought possible
failures of medication

doubts of another's existence
—tell it over and over, the words
get thick with unmeaning—
yet never have we been closer to the truth
of the lies we were living, listen to me:
the faithfulness I can imagine would be a weed
flowering in tar, a blue energy piercing
the massed atoms of a bedrock disbelief.

1971

WAKING IN THE DARK

1.

The thing that arrests me is
        how we are composed of molecules

    (he showed me the figure in the paving stones)

arranged without our knowledge and consent

                like the wirephoto composed
                of millions of dots

                in which the man from Bangladesh
                walks starving
                            on the front page
                            knowing nothing about it

        which is his presence for the world

2.

We were standing in line outside of something
two by two, or alone in pairs, or simply alone,
looking into windows full of scissors,
windows full of shoes. The street was closing,
the city was closing, would we be the lucky ones
to make it? They were showing
in a glass case, the Man Without A Country.
We held up our passports in his face, we wept for him.

They are dumping animal blood into the sea
to bring up the sharks. Sometimes every
aperture of my body
leaks blood. I don't know whether
to pretend that this is natural.
Is there a law about this, a law of nature?
You worship the blood
you call it hysterical bleeding
you want to drink it like milk
you dip your finger into it and write
you faint at the smell of it
you dream of dumping me into the sea.

3.

The tragedy of sex
lies around us, a woodlot
the axes are sharpened for.
The old shelters and huts
stare through the clearing with a certain resolution
—the hermit's cabin, the hunters' shack—
scenes of masturbation
and dirty jokes.

A man's world. But finished.
They themselves have sold it to the machines.
I walk the unconscious forest,
a woman dressed in old army fatigues
that have shrunk to fit her, I am lost
at moments, I feel dazed
by the sun pawing between the trees,
cold in the bog and lichen of the thicket.
Nothing will save this. I am alone,
kicking the last rotting logs
with their strange smell of life, not death,
wondering what on earth it all might have become.

4.

Clarity,
        spray

blinding and purging

spears of sun striking the water

the bodies riding the air
like gliders

the bodies in slow motion

falling
into the pool
at the Berlin Olympics

control; loss of control

the bodies rising
arching back to the tower
time reeling backward

clarity of open air
before the dark chambers
with the shower-heads

the bodies falling again
freely

               faster than light
the water opening
like air
like realization

A woman made this film
against

the law
of gravity

5.

All night dreaming of a body
space weighs on differently from mine
We are making love in the street
the traffic flows off from us
pouring back like a sheet
the asphalt stirs with tenderness
there is no dismay
we move together like underwater plants

Over and over, starting to wake
I dive back to discover you
still whispering, *touch me,* we go on
streaming through the slow
citylight forest ocean
stirring our body hair

But this is the saying of a dream
on waking
I wish there were somewhere
actual we could stand
handing the power-glasses back and forth
looking at the earth, the wildwood
where the split began

1971

INCIPIENCE

1.   To live, to lie awake
under scarred plaster
while ice is forming over the earth
at an hour when nothing can be done
to further any decision

to know the composing of the thread
inside the spider's body
first atoms of the web
visible tomorrow

to feel the fiery future
of every matchstick in the kitchen

Nothing can be done
but by inches. I write out my life
hour by hour, word by word
gazing into the anger of old women on the bus
numbering the striations
of air inside the ice cube
imagining the existence
of something uncreated
this poem
our lives

2.   A man is asleep in the next room
        We are his dreams
        We have the heads and breasts of women
        the bodies of birds of prey
        Sometimes we turn into silver serpents
While we sit up smoking and talking of how to live
he turns on the bed and murmurs

A man is asleep in the next room
        A neurosurgeon enters his dream
        and begins to dissect his brain
        She does not look like a nurse
        she is absorbed in her work
        she has a stern, delicate face like Marie Curie
She is not/might be either of us

A man is asleep in the next room
        He has spent a whole day
        standing, throwing stones into the black pool
        which keeps its blackness
Outside the frame of his dream we are stumbling up the hill
        hand in hand, stumbling and guiding each other
        over the scarred volcanic rock

1971

117

THE STRANGER

Looking as I've looked before, straight down the heart
of the street to the river
walking the rivers of the avenues
feeling the shudder of the caves beneath the asphalt
watching the lights turn on in the towers
walking as I've walked before
like a man, like a woman, in the city
my visionary anger cleansing my sight
and the detailed perceptions of mercy
flowering from that anger

if I come into a room out of the sharp misty light
and hear them talking a dead language
if they ask me my identity
what can I say but
I am the androgyne
I am the living mind you fail to describe
in your dead language
the lost noun, the verb surviving
only in the infinitive
the letters of my name are written under the lids
of the newborn child

1972

SONG

You're wondering if I'm lonely:
OK then, yes, I'm lonely
as a plane rides lonely and level
on its radio beam, aiming
across the Rockies
for the blue-strung aisles
of an airfield on the ocean

You want to ask, am I lonely?
Well, of course, lonely
as a woman driving across country
day after day, leaving behind
mile after mile
little towns she might have stopped
and lived and died in, lonely

If I'm lonely
it must be the loneliness
of waking first, of breathing
dawn's first cold breath on the city
of being the one awake
in a house wrapped in sleep

If I'm lonely
it's with the rowboat ice-fast on the shore
in the last red light of the year
that knows what it is, that knows it's neither
ice nor mud nor winter light
but wood, with a gift for burning

1971

119

DIVING INTO THE WRECK

First having read the book of myths,
and loaded the camera,
and checked the edge of the knife-blade,
I put on
the body-armor of black rubber
the absurd flippers
the grave and awkward mask.
I am having to do this
not like Cousteau with his
assiduous team
aboard the sun-flooded schooner
but here alone.

There is a ladder.
The ladder is always there
hanging innocently
close to the side of the schooner.
We know what it is for,
we who have used it.
Otherwise
it's a piece of maritime floss
some sundry equipment.

I go down.
Rung after rung and still
the oxygen immerses me
the blue light
the clear atoms
of our human air.
I go down.
My flippers cripple me,
I crawl like an insect down the ladder
and there is no one

to tell me when the ocean
will begin.

First the air is blue and then
it is bluer and then green and then
black I am blacking out and yet
my mask is powerful
it pumps my blood with power
the sea is another story
the sea is not a question of power
I have to learn alone
to turn my body without force
in the deep element.

And now: it is easy to forget
what I came for
among so many who have always
lived here
swaying their crenellated fans
between the reefs
and besides
you breathe differently down here.

I came to explore the wreck.
The words are purposes.
The words are maps.
I came to see the damage that was done
and the treasures that prevail.
I stroke the beam of my lamp
slowly along the flank
of something more permanent
than fish or weed

the thing I came for:
the wreck and not the story of the wreck
the thing itself and not the myth
the drowned face always staring
toward the sun
the evidence of damage
worn by salt and sway into this threadbare beauty
the ribs of the disaster
curving their assertion
among the tentative haunters.

This is the place.
And I am here, the mermaid whose dark hair
streams black, the merman in his armored body
We circle silently
about the wreck
we dive into the hold.
I am she: I am he

whose drowned face sleeps with open eyes
whose breasts still bear the stress
whose silver, copper, vermeil cargo lies
obscurely inside barrels
half-wedged and left to rot
we are the half-destroyed instruments
that once held to a course
the water-eaten log
the fouled compass

We are, I am, you are
by cowardice or courage
the one who find our way
back to this scene
carrying a knife, a camera

a book of myths
in which
our names do not appear.

1972

THE PHENOMENOLOGY OF ANGER

1. The freedom of the wholly mad
to smear & play with her madness
write with her fingers dipped in it
the length of a room

which is not, of course, the freedom
you have, walking on Broadway
to stop & turn back or go on
10 blocks; 20 blocks

but feels enviable maybe
to the compromised

curled in the placenta of the real
which was to feed & which is strangling her.

2. Trying to light a log that's lain in the damp
as long as this house has stood:
even with dry sticks I can't get started
even with thorns.
I twist last year into a knot of old headlines
—this rose won't bloom.

How does a pile of rags the machinist wiped his hands on
feel in its cupboard, hour upon hour?
Each day during the heat-wave
they took the temperature of the haymow.
I huddled fugitive
in the warm sweet simmer of the hay

muttering: *Come.*

3. Flat heartland of winter.
The moonmen come back from the moon
the firemen come out of the fire.
Time without a taste: time without decisions.

Self-hatred, a monotone in the mind.
The shallowness of a life lived in exile
even in the hot countries.
Cleaver, staring into a window full of knives.

4. White light splits the room.
Table.   Window.   Lampshade.   You.

My hands, sticky in a new way.
Menstrual blood
seeming to leak from your side.

Will the judges try to tell me
which was the blood of whom?

5. Madness.   Suicide.   Murder.
Is there no way out but these?
The enemy, always just out of sight
snowshoeing the next forest, shrouded
in a snowy blur, abominable snowman
—at once the most destructive

and the most elusive being
gunning down the babies at My Lai
vanishing in the face of confrontation.

The prince of air and darkness
computing body counts, masturbating
in the factory
of facts.

6. Fantasies of murder: not enough:
to kill is to cut off from pain
but the killer goes on hurting

Not enough. When I dream of meeting
the enemy, this is my dream:

white acetylene
ripples from my body
effortlessly released
perfectly trained
on the true enemy

raking his body down to the thread
of existence
burning away his lie
leaving him in a new
world; a changed
man

7. I suddenly see the world
as no longer viable:
you are out there burning the crops
with some new sublimate
This morning you left the bed
we still share

and went out to spread impotence
upon the world

I hate you.
I hate the mask you wear, your eyes
assuming a depth
they do not possess, drawing me
into the grotto of your skull
the landscape of bone
I hate your words
they make me think of fake
revolutionary bills
crisp imitation parchment
they sell at battlefields.

Last night, in this room, weeping
I asked you: *what are you feeling?*
do you feel anything?

Now in the torsion of your body
as you defoliate the fields we lived from
I have your answer.

8. Dogeared earth. Wormeaten moon.
A pale cross-hatching of silver
lies like a wire screen on the black
water. All these phenomena
are temporary.

I would have loved to live in a world
of women and men gaily
in collusion with green leaves, stalks,
building mineral cities, transparent domes,
little huts of woven grass
each with its own pattern—

a conspiracy to coexist
with the Crab Nebula, the exploding
universe, the Mind—

9. *The only real love I have ever felt*
was for children and other women.
Everything else was lust, pity,
self-hatred, pity, lust.
This is a woman's confession.
Now, look again at the face
of Botticelli's Venus, Kali,
the Judith of Chartres
with her so-called smile.

10. how we are burning up our lives
testimony:

> the subway
> hurtling to Brooklyn
> her head on her knees
> asleep or drugged

la vía del tren subterráneo
es peligrosa

> many sleep
> the whole way
> others sit
> staring holes of fire into the air
> others plan rebellion:
> night after night
> awake in prison, my mind
> licked at the mattress like a flame
> till the cellblock went up roaring

> Thoreau setting fire to the woods

Every act of becoming conscious
(it says here in this book)
is an unnatural act

1972

MERCED

Fantasies of old age:
they have rounded us up
in a rest-camp for the outworn.
Somewhere in some dustbowl
a barbed-wire cantonment
of low-cost dustcolored prefab
buildings, smelling of shame
and hopeless incontinence
identical clothes of disposable
paper, identical rations
of chemically flavored food
Death in order, by gas,
hypodermics daily
to neutralize despair
So I imagine my world
in my seventieth year alive
and outside the barbed wire
a purposeless exchange
of consciousness for the absence
of pain. We will call this life.

Yet only last summer I
burned my feet in the sand
of that valley traced by the thread

of the cold quick river Merced
watered by plummets of white
When I swam, my body ached
from the righteous cold
when I lay back floating the jays
flittered from pine to pine
and the shade moved hour by hour
across El Capitan
Our wine cooled in the water
and I watched my sons, half-men
half-children, testing their part
in a world almost archaic
so precious by this time
that merely to step in pure water
or stare into clear air
is to feel a spasm of pain.

For weeks now a rage
has possessed my body, driving
now out upon men and women
now inward upon myself
Walking Amsterdam Avenue
I find myself in tears
without knowing which thought
forced water to my eyes
To speak to another human
becomes a risk
I think of Norman Morrison
the Buddhists of Saigon
the black teacher last week
who put himself to death
to waken guilt in hearts
too numb to get the message
in a world masculinity made
unfit for women or men

Taking off in a plane
I look down at the city
which meant life to me, not death
and think that somewhere there
a cold center, composed
of pieces of human beings
metabolized, restructured
by a process they do not feel
is spreading in our midst
and taking over our minds
a thing that feels neither guilt
nor rage: that is unable
to hate, therefore to love.

1972

LIVING IN THE CAVE

Reading the Parable of the Cave
While living in the cave,

                         black moss
deadening my footsteps
candles stuck on rock-ledges
weakening my eyes

These things around me, with their
daily requirements:

                    fill me, empty me
talk to me, warm me, let me
suck on you

Every one of them has a plan that depends on me

stalactites want to become
stalagmites
veins of ore
imagine their preciousness

candles see themselves disembodied
into gas
and taking flight

the bat hangs dreaming
of an airy world

None of them, not one
sees me
as I see them

1972

FOR THE DEAD

I dreamed I called you on the telephone
to say: *Be kinder to yourself*
but you were sick and would not answer

The waste of my love goes on this way
trying to save you from yourself

I have always wondered about the leftover
energy, water rushing down a hill
long after the rains have stopped

or the fire you want to go to bed from
but cannot leave, burning-down but not burnt-down
the red coals more extreme, more curious
in their flashing and dying
than you wish they were
sitting there long after midnight

1972

FROM A SURVIVOR

The pact that we made was the ordinary pact
of men & women in those days

I don't know who we thought we were
that our personalities
could resist the failures of the race

Lucky or unlucky, we didn't know
the race had failures of that order
and that we were going to share them

Like everybody else, we thought of ourselves as special

Your body is as vivid to me
as it ever was: even more

since my feeling for it is clearer:
I know what it could do and could not do

it is no longer
the body of a god
or anything with power over my life

Next year it would have been 20 years
and you are wastefully dead
who might have made the leap
we talked, too late, of making

which I live now
not as a leap
but a succession of brief, amazing movements

each one making possible the next

1972

from

POEMS

(1975)

FROM AN OLD HOUSE IN AMERICA

1.

Deliberately, long ago
the carcasses

of old bugs crumbled
into the rut of the window

and we started sleeping here
Fresh June bugs batter this June's

screens, June-lightning batters
the spiderweb

I sweep the wood-dust
from the wood-box

the snout of the vacuum cleaner
sucks the past away

2.

Other lives were lived here:
mostly un-articulate

yet someone left her creamy signature
in the trail of rusticated

narcissus straggling up
through meadowgrass and vetch

Families breathed close
boxed-in from the cold

hard times, short growing season
the old rainwater cistern
hulks in the cellar

3.

Like turning through the contents of a drawer:
these rusted screws, this empty vial

useless, this box of watercolor paints
dried to insolubility—

but this—
this pack of cards with no card missing

still playable
and three good fuses

and this toy: a little truck
scarred red, yet all its wheels still turn

The humble tenacity of things
waiting for people, waiting for months, for years

4.

Often rebuked, yet always back returning
I place my hand on the hand

of the dead, invisible palm-print
on the doorframe

spiked with daylilies, green leaves
catching in the screen door

or I read the backs of old postcards
curling from thumbtacks, winter and summer

fading through cobweb-tinted panes—
white church in Norway

Dutch hyacinths bleeding azure
red beach on Corsica

set-pieces of the world
stuck to this house of plank

I flash on wife and husband
embattled, in the years

that dried, dim ink was wet
those signatures

5.

If they call me man-hater, you
would have known it for a lie

but the *you* I want to speak to
has become your death

If I dream of you these days
I know my dreams are mine and not of you

yet something hangs between us
older and stranger than ourselves

like a translucent curtain, a sheet of water
a dusty window

the irreducible, incomplete connection
between the dead and living

or between man and woman in this
savagely fathered and unmothered world

6.

The other side of a translucent
curtain, a sheet of water

a dusty window, Non-being
utters its flat tones

the speech of an actor learning his lines
phonetically

the final autistic statement
of the self-destroyer

All my energy reaches out tonight
to comprehend a miracle beyond

raising the dead: the undead to watch
back on the road of birth

7.

I am an American woman:
I turn that over

like a leaf pressed in a book
I stop and look up from

into the coals of the stove
or the black square of the window

Foot-slogging through the Bering Strait
jumping from the *Arbella* to my death

chained to the corpse beside me
I feel my pains begin

I am washed up on this continent
shipped here to be fruitful

my body a hollow ship
bearing sons to the wilderness

sons who ride away
on horseback, daughters

whose juices drain like mine
into the *arroyo* of stillbirths, massacres

Hanged as witches, sold as breeding-wenches
my sisters leave me

I am not the wheatfield
nor the virgin forest

I never chose this place
yet I am of it now

In my decent collar, in the daguerreotype
I pierce its legend with my look

my hands wring the necks of prairie chickens
I am used to blood

When the men hit the hobo track
I stay on with the children

my power is brief and local
but I know my power

I have lived in isolation
from other women, so much

in the mining camps, the first cities
the Great Plains winters

Most of the time, in my sex, I was alone

8.

Tonight in this northeast kingdom
striated iris stand in a jar with daisies

the porcupine gnaws in the shed
fireflies beat and simmer

caterpillars begin again
their long, innocent climb

the length of leaves of burdock
or webbing of a garden chair

plain and ordinary things
speak softly

the light square on old wallpaper
where a poster has fallen down

Robert Indiana's LOVE
leftover of a decade

9.

I do not want to simplify
Or: I would simplify

by naming the complexity
It was made over-simple all along

the separation of powers
the allotment of sufferings

her spine cracking in labor
his plow driving across the Indian graves

her hand unconscious on the cradle, her mind
with the wild geese

his mother-hatred driving him
into exile from the earth

the refugee couple with their cardboard luggage
standing on the ramshackle landing-stage

he with fingers frozen around his Law
she with her down quilt sewn through iron nights

—the weight of the old world, plucked
drags after them, a random feather-bed

10.

Her children dead of diphtheria, she
set herself on fire with kerosene

(O Lord I was unworthy
Thou didst find me out)

she left the kitchen scrubbed
down to the marrow of its boards

"The penalty for barrenness
is emptiness

my punishment is my crime
what I have failed to do, is me . . ."

—Another month without a show
and this the seventh year

O Father let this thing pass out of me
I swear to You

I will live for the others, asking nothing
I will ask nothing, ever, for myself

11.

Out back of this old house
datura tangles with a gentler weed

its spiked pods smelling
of bad dreams and death

I reach through the dark, groping
past spines of nightmare

to brush the leaves of sensuality
A dream of tenderness

wrestles with all I know of history
I cannot now lie down

with a man who fears my power
or reaches for me as for death

or with a lover who imagines
we are not in danger

12.

If it was lust that had defined us—
their lust and fear of our deep places

we have done our time
as faceless torsos licked by fire

we are in the open, on our way—
our counterparts

the pinyon jay, the small
gilt-winged insect

the Cessna throbbing level
the raven floating in the gorge

the rose and violet vulva of the earth
filling with darkness

yet deep within a single sparkle
of red, a human fire

and near and yet above the western planet
calmly biding her time

13.

They were the distractions, lust and fear
but are

themselves a key
Everything that can be used, will be:

the fathers in their ceremonies
the genital contests

the cleansing of blood from pubic hair
the placenta buried and guarded

their terror of blinding
by the look of her who bore them

If you do not believe
that fear and hatred

read the lesson again
in the old dialect

14.

But can't you see me as a human being
he said

What is a human being
she said

I try to understand
he said

what will you undertake
she said

will you punish me for history
he said

what will you undertake
she said

do you believe in collective guilt
he said

let me look in your eyes
she said

15.

Who is here. The Erinyes.
One to sit in judgment.

One to speak tenderness.
One to inscribe the verdict on the canyon wall.

If you have not confessed
the damage

if you have not recognized
the Mother of reparations

if you have not come to terms
with the women in the mirror

if you have not come to terms
with the inscription

the terms of the ordeal
the discipline   the verdict

if still you are on your way
still She awaits your coming

16.

"Such women are dangerous
to the order of things"

and yes, we will be dangerous
to ourselves

groping through spines of nightmare
(*datura* tangling with a simpler herb)

because the line dividing
lucidity from darkness

is yet to be marked out

Isolation, the dream
of the frontier woman

leveling her rifle along
the homestead fence

still snares our pride
—a suicidal leaf

laid under the burning-glass
in the sun's eye

Any woman's death diminishes me

1974

THE FACT OF A DOORFRAME

means there is something to hold
onto with both hands
while slowly thrusting my forehead against the wood
and taking it away
one of the oldest motions of suffering
as Makeba sings
a courage-song for warriors
music is suffering made powerful

I think of the story
of the goose-girl who passed through the high gate
where the head of her favorite mare

was nailed to the arch
and in a human voice
If she could see thee now, thy mother's heart would break
said the head
of Falada

Now, again, poetry,
violent, arcane, common,
hewn of the commonest living substance
into archway, portal, frame
I grasp for you, your bloodstained splinters, your
ancient and stubborn poise
—as the earth trembles—
burning out from the grain

1974

from

THE DREAM
OF A COMMON
LANGUAGE

(1978)

I go where I love and where I am loved,
into the snow;

I go to the things I love
with no thought of duty or pity
                    —H. D., *The Flowering of the Rod*

POWER

Living   in the earth-deposits   of our history

Today a backhoe divulged   out of a crumbling flank of earth
one bottle   amber   perfect   a hundred-year-old
cure for fever   or melancholy   a tonic
for living on this earth   in the winters of this climate

Today I was reading about Marie Curie:
she must have known she suffered   from radiation sickness
her body bombarded for years   by the element
she had purified
It seems she denied to the end
the source of the cataracts on her eyes
the cracked and suppurating skin   of her finger-ends
till she could no longer hold   a test-tube or a pencil

She died   a famous woman   denying
her wounds
denying
her wounds   came   from the same source as her power

1974

PHANTASIA FOR ELVIRA SHATAYEV

*(Leader of a women's climbing team, all of whom died in a
storm on Lenin Peak, August 1974. Later, Shatayev's
husband found and buried the bodies.)*

The cold felt cold until our blood
grew colder   then the wind
died down and we slept

If in this sleep I speak
It's with a voice no longer personal
(I want to say   *with voices*)
When the wind tore   our breath from us at last
we had no need of words
For months   for years   each one of us
had felt her own *yes*   growing in her
slowly forming   as she stood at windows   waited
for trains   mended her rucksack   combed her hair
What we were to learn   was simply   what we had
up here   as out of all words   that *yes*   gathered
its forces   fused itself   and only just in time
to meet a *No* of no degrees
the black hole   sucking the world in

I feel you climbing toward me
your cleated bootsoles leaving   their geometric bite
colossally embossed   on microscopic crystals
as when I trailed you in the Caucasus
Now I am further
ahead   than either of us dreamed   anyone would be
I have become

the white snow packed like asphalt by the wind
the women I love   lightly flung   against the mountain
that blue sky
our frozen eyes unribboned   through the storm
we could have stitched that blueness   together   like a quilt

You come (I know this)   with your love   your loss
strapped to your body   with your tape-recorder   camera
ice-pick   against advisement
to give us burial in the snow   and in your mind
While my body lies out here
flashing like a prism   into your eyes

how could you sleep   You climbed here for yourself
we climbed for ourselves

When you have buried us   told your story
ours does not end   we stream
into the unfinished   the unbegun
the possible
Every cell's core of heat   pulsed out of us
into the thin air   of the universe
the armature of rock beneath these snows
this mountain   which has taken   the imprint of our minds
through changes elemental and minute
as those we underwent
to bring each other here
choosing ourselves   each other   and this life
whose every breath   and grasp   and further foothold
is somewhere   still enacted   and continuing

In the diary I wrote: *Now we are ready*
and each of us knows it   I have never loved
like this   I have never seen
my own forces so taken up and shared
and given back
After the long training   the early sieges
we are moving almost effortlessly in our love

In the diary as the wind   began to tear
at the tents over us   I wrote:
We know now we have always been in danger
down in our separateness
and now up here together   but till now
we had not touched our strength

In the diary torn from my fingers I had written:
What does love mean

What does it mean   "to survive"
A cable of blue fire ropes our bodies
burning together in the snow   We will not live
to settle for less   We have dreamed of this
all of our lives

1974

SPLITTINGS

1.

My body opens over San Francisco like the day-
light raining down   each pore crying the change of light
I am not with her   I have been waking off and on
all night to that pain   not simply absence but
the presence of the past   destructive
to living here and now   Yet if I could instruct
myself, if we could learn to learn from pain
even as it grasps us   if the mind, the mind that lives
in this body could refuse   to let itself be crushed
in that grasp   it would loosen   Pain would have to stand
off from me and listen   its dark breath still on me
but the mind could begin to speak to pain
and pain would have to answer:

                                We are older now
we have met before   these are my hands before your eyes
my figure blotting out   all that is not mine
I am the pain of division   creator of divisions
it is I who blot your lover from you

and not the time-zones nor the miles
It is not separation calls me forth   but I
who am separation   And remember
I have no existence   apart from you

2.

I believe I am choosing something new
not to suffer uselessly   yet still to feel
Does the infant memorize the body of the mother
and create her in absence?   or simply cry
primordial loneliness?   does the bed of the stream
once diverted   mourning   remember wetness?
But we, we live so much in these
configurations of the past   I choose
to separate her   from my past we have not shared
I choose not to suffer uselessly
to detect primordial pain as it stalks toward me
flashing its bleak torch in my eyes   blotting out
her particular being   the details of her love
I will not be divided   from her or from myself
by myths of separation
while her mind and body in Manhattan are more with me
than the smell of eucalyptus coolly burning   on these hills

3.

The world tells me I am its creature
I am raked by eyes   brushed by hands
I want to crawl into her for refuge   lay my head
in the space   between her breast and shoulder
abnegating power for love
as women have done   or hiding

from power in her love   like a man
I refuse these givens   the splitting
between love and action   I am choosing
not to suffer uselessly   and not to use her
I choose to love   this time   for once
with all my intelligence

1974

TO A POET

Ice splits   under the metal
shovel   another day
hazed light off fogged panes
cruelty of winter   landlocked   your life
wrapped round you   in your twenties
an old bathrobe   dragged down
with milkstains   tearstains   dust

Scraping eggcrust from the child's
dried dish   skimming the skin
from cooled milk   wringing diapers
Language floats at the vanishing-point
incarnate   breathes the fluorescent bulb
primary   states the scarred grain of the floor
and on the ceiling in torn plaster laughs   *imago*

> *and I have fears that you will cease to be*
> *before your pen has glean'd your teeming brain*

for you are not a suicide
but no-one calls this murder
Small mouths, needy, suck you: *This is love*

I write this   not for you
who fight to write your own
words   fighting up the falls
but for another woman   dumb
with loneliness   dust   seeping plastic bags
with children in a house
where language floats and spins
abortion   in
the bowl

1974

CARTOGRAPHIES OF SILENCE

1.

A conversation begins
with a lie. And each

speaker of the so-called common language feels
the ice-floe split, the drift apart

as if powerless, as if up against
a force of nature

A poem can begin
with a lie. And be torn up.

A conversation has other laws
recharges itself with its own

false energy. Cannot be torn
up. Infiltrates our blood. Repeats itself.

Inscribes with its unreturning stylus
the isolation it denies.

2.

The classical music station
playing hour upon hour in the apartment

the picking up and picking up
and again picking up the telephone

The syllables uttering
the old script over and over

The loneliness of the liar
living in the formal network of the lie

twisting the dials to drown the terror
beneath the unsaid word

3.

The technology of silence
The rituals, etiquette

the blurring of terms
silence not absence

of words or music or even
raw sounds

Silence can be a plan
rigorously executed

the blueprint to a life

It is a presence
it has a history a   form

Do not confuse it
with any kind of absence

4.

How calm, how inoffensive these words
begin to seem to me

though begun in grief and anger
Can I break through this film of the abstract

without wounding myself or you
there is enough pain here

This is why the classical or the jazz music station plays?
to give a ground of meaning to our pain?

5.

The silence that strips bare:
In Dreyer's *Passion of Joan*

Falconetti's face, hair shorn, a great geography
mutely surveyed by the camera

If there were a poetry where this could happen
not as blank spaces or as words

stretched like a skin over meanings
but as silence falls at the end

of a night through which two people
have talked till dawn

6.

The scream
of an illegitimate voice

It has ceased to hear itself, therefore
it asks itself

How dó I exist?

This was the silence I wanted to break in you
I had questions but you would not answer

I had answers but you could not use them
This is useless to you and perhaps to others

7.

It was an old theme even for me:
Language cannot do everything—

chalk it on the walls where the dead poets
lie in their mausoleums

If at the will of the poet the poem
could turn into a thing

a granite flank laid bare, a lifted head
alight with dew

If it could simply look you in the face
with naked eyeballs, not letting you turn

till you, and I who long to make this thing,
were finally clarified together in its stare

8.

No. Let me have this dust,
these pale clouds dourly lingering, these words

moving with ferocious accuracy
like the blind child's fingers

or the newborn infant's mouth
violent with hunger

No one can give me, I have long ago
taken this method

whether of bran pouring from the loose-woven sack
or of the bunsen-flame turned low and blue

If from time to time I envy
the pure annunciations to the eye

the *visio beatifica*
if from time to time I long to turn

163

like the Eleusinian hierophant
holding up a simple ear of grain

for return to the concrete and everlasting world
what in fact I keep choosing

are these words, these whispers, conversations
from which time after time the truth breaks moist and green.

1975

TWENTY-ONE LOVE POEMS

I

Wherever in this city, screens flicker
with pornography, with science-fiction vampires,
victimized hirelings bending to the lash,
we also have to walk . . . if simply as we walk
through the rainsoaked garbage, the tabloid cruelties
of our own neighborhoods.
We need to grasp our lives inseparable
from those rancid dreams, that blurt of metal, those disgraces,
and the red begonia perilously flashing
from a tenement sill six stories high,
or the long-legged young girls playing ball
in the junior highschool playground.
No one has imagined us. We want to live like trees,
sycamores blazing through the sulfuric air,
dappled with scars, still exuberantly budding,
our animal passion rooted in the city.

II

I wake up in your bed. I know I have been dreaming.
Much earlier, the alarm broke us from each other,
you've been at your desk for hours. I know what I dreamed:
our friend the poet comes into my room
where I've been writing for days,
drafts, carbons, poems are scattered everywhere,
and I want to show her one poem
which is the poem of my life. But I hesitate,
and wake. You've kissed my hair
to wake me. *I dreamed you were a poem,*
I say, *a poem I wanted to show someone* . . .
and I laugh and fall dreaming again
of the desire to show you to everyone I love,

to move openly together
in the pull of gravity, which is not simple,
which carries the feathered grass a long way down the upbreathing air.

III

Since we're not young, weeks have to do time
for years of missing each other. Yet only this odd warp
in time tells me we're not young.
Did I ever walk the morning streets at twenty,
my limbs streaming with a purer joy?
did I lean from any window over the city
listening for the future
as I listen here with nerves tuned for your ring?
And you, you move toward me with the same tempo.
Your eyes are everlasting, the green spark
of the blue-eyed grass of early summer,
the green-blue wild cress washed by the spring.
At twenty, yes: we thought we'd live forever.
At forty-five, I want to know even our limits.
I touch you knowing we weren't born tomorrow,
and somehow, each of us will help the other live,
and somewhere, each of us must help the other die.

IV

I come home from you through the early light of spring
flashing off ordinary walls, the Pez Dorado,
the Discount Wares, the shoe-store. . . . I'm lugging my sack
of groceries, I dash for the elevator
where a man, taut, elderly, carefully composed
lets the door almost close on me.—*For god's sake hold it!*
I croak at him.—*Hysterical,*—he breathes my way.

I let myself into the kitchen, unload my bundles,
make coffee, open the window, put on Nina Simone
singing *Here comes the sun.* . . . I open the mail,
drinking delicious coffee, delicious music,
my body still both light and heavy with you. The mail
lets fall a Xerox of something written by a man
aged 27, a hostage, tortured in prison:
My genitals have been the object of such a sadistic display
they keep me constantly awake with the pain . . .
Do whatever you can to survive.
You know, I think that men love wars . . .
And my incurable anger, my unmendable wounds
break open further with tears, I am crying helplessly,
and they still control the world, and you are not in my arms.

V

This apartment full of books could crack open
to the thick jaws, the bulging eyes
of monsters, easily: Once open the books, you have to face
the underside of everything you've loved—
the rack and pincers held in readiness, the gag
even the best voices have had to mumble through,
the silence burying unwanted children—
women, deviants, witnesses—in desert sand.
Kenneth tells me he's been arranging his books
so he can look at Blake and Kafka while he types;
yes; and we still have to reckon with Swift
loathing the woman's flesh while praising her mind,
Goethe's dread of the Mothers, Claudel vilifying Gide,
and the ghosts—their hands clasped for centuries—
of artists dying in childbirth, wise-women charred at the stake,
centuries of books unwritten piled behind these shelves;
and we still have to stare into the absence

of men who would not, women who could not, speak
to our life—this still unexcavated hole
called civilization, this act of translation, this half-world.

VI

Your small hands, precisely equal to my own—
only the thumb is larger, longer—in these hands
I could trust the world, or in many hands like these,
handling power-tools or steering-wheel
or touching a human face. . . . Such hands could turn
the unborn child rightways in the birth canal
or pilot the exploratory rescue-ship
through icebergs, or piece together
the fine, needle-like sherds of a great krater-cup
bearing on its sides
figures of ecstatic women striding
to the sibyl's den or the Eleusinian cave—
such hands might carry out an unavoidable violence
with such restraint, with such a grasp
of the range and limits of violence
that violence ever after would be obsolete.

VII

What kind of beast would turn its life into words?
What atonement is this all about?
—and yet, writing words like these, I'm also living.
Is all this close to the wolverines' howled signals,
that modulated cantata of the wild?
or, when away from you I try to create you in words,
am I simply using you, like a river or a war?
And how have I used rivers, how have I used wars

to escape writing of the worst thing of all—
not the crimes of others, not even our own death,
but the failure to want our freedom passionately enough
so that blighted elms, sick rivers, massacres would seem
mere emblems of that desecration of ourselves?

VIII

I can see myself years back at Sunion,
hurting with an infected foot, Philoctetes
in woman's form, limping the long path,
lying on a headland over the dark sea,
looking down the red rocks to where a soundless curl
of white told me a wave had struck,
imagining the pull of that water from that height,
knowing deliberate suicide wasn't my métier,
yet all the time nursing, measuring that wound.
Well, that's finished. The woman who cherished
her suffering is dead. I am her descendant.
I love the scar-tissue she handed on to me,
but I want to go on from here with you
fighting the temptation to make a career of pain.

IX

Your silence today is a pond where drowned things live
I want to see raised dripping and brought into the sun.
It's not my own face I see there, but other faces,
even your face at another age.
Whatever's lost there is needed by both of us—
a watch of old gold, a water-blurred fever chart,
a key. . . . Even the silt and pebbles of the bottom
deserve their glint of recognition. I fear this silence,

this inarticulate life. I'm waiting
for a wind that will gently open this sheeted water
for once, and show me what I can do
for you, who have often made the unnameable
nameable for others, even for me.

X

Your dog, tranquil and innocent, dozes through
our cries, our murmured dawn conspiracies
our telephone calls. She knows—what can she know?
If in my human arrogance I claim to read
her eyes, I find there only my own animal thoughts:
that creatures must find each other for bodily comfort,
that voices of the psyche drive through the flesh
further than the dense brain could have foretold,
that the planetary nights are growing cold for those
on the same journey who want to touch
one creature-traveler clear to the end;
that without tenderness, we are in hell.

XI

Every peak is a crater. This is the law of volcanoes,
making them eternally and visibly female.
No height without depth, without a burning core,
though our straw soles shred on the hardened lava.
I want to travel with you to every sacred mountain
smoking within like the sibyl stooped over her tripod,
I want to reach for your hand as we scale the path,
to feel your arteries glowing in my clasp,
never failing to note the small, jewel-like flower
unfamiliar to us, nameless till we rename her,

that clings to the slowly altering rock—
that detail outside ourselves that brings us to ourselves,
was here before us, knew we would come, and sees beyond us.

XII

Sleeping, turning in turn like planets
rotating in their midnight meadow:
a touch is enough to let us know
we're not alone in the universe, even in sleep:
the dream-ghosts of two worlds
walking their ghost-towns, almost address each other.
I've wakened to your muttered words
spoken light- or dark-years away
as if my own voice had spoken.
But we have different voices, even in sleep,
and our bodies, so alike, are yet so different
and the past echoing through our bloodstreams
is freighted with different language, different meanings—
though in any chronicle of the world we share
it could be written with new meaning
we were two lovers of one gender,
we were two women of one generation.

XIII

The rules break like a thermometer,
quicksilver spills across the charted systems,
we're out in a country that has no language
no laws, we're chasing the raven and the wren
through gorges unexplored since dawn
whatever we do together is pure invention
the maps they gave us were out of date

by years . . . we're driving through the desert
wondering if the water will hold out
the hallucinations turn to simple villages
the music on the radio comes clear—
neither *Rosenkavalier* nor *Götterdämmerung*
but a woman's voice singing old songs
with new words, with a quiet bass, a flute
plucked and fingered by women outside the law.

XIV

It was your vision of the pilot
confirmed my vision of you: you said, *He keeps
on steering headlong into the waves, on purpose*
while we crouched in the open hatchway
vomiting into plastic bags
for three hours between St. Pierre and Miquelon.
I never felt closer to you.
In the close cabin where the honeymoon couples
huddled in each other's laps and arms
I put my hand on your thigh
to comfort both of us, your hand came over mine,
we stayed that way, suffering together
in our bodies, as if all suffering
were physical, we touched so in the presence
of strangers who knew nothing and cared less
vomiting their private pain
as if all suffering were physical.

(THE FLOATING POEM, UNNUMBERED)

Whatever happens with us, your body
will haunt mine—tender, delicate

your lovemaking, like the half-curled frond
of the fiddlehead fern in forests
just washed by sun. Your traveled, generous thighs
between which my whole face has come and come—
the innocence and wisdom of the place my tongue has found there—
the live, insatiate dance of your nipples in my mouth—
your touch on me, firm, protective, searching
me out, your strong tongue and slender fingers
reaching where I had been waiting years for you
in my rose-wet cave—whatever happens, this is.

XV

If I lay on that beach with you
white, empty, pure green water warmed by the Gulf Stream
and lying on that beach we could not stay
because the wind drove fine sand against us
as if it were against us
if we tried to withstand it and we failed—
if we drove to another place
to sleep in each other's arms
and the beds were narrow like prisoners' cots
and we were tired and did not sleep together
and this was what we found, so this is what we did—
was the failure ours?
If I cling to circumstances I could feel
not responsible. Only she who says
she did not choose, is the loser in the end.

XVI

Across a city from you, I'm with you,
just as an August night

moony, inlet-warm, seabathed, I watched you sleep,
the scrubbed, sheenless wood of the dressing-table
cluttered with our brushes, books, vials in the moonlight—
or a salt-mist orchard, lying at your side
watching red sunset through the screendoor of the cabin,
G minor Mozart on the tape-recorder,
falling asleep to the music of the sea.
This island of Manhattan is wide enough
for both of us, and narrow:
I can hear your breath tonight, I know how your face
lies upturned, the halflight tracing
your generous, delicate mouth
where grief and laughter sleep together.

XVII

No one's fated or doomed to love anyone.
The accidents happen, we're not heroines,
they happen in our lives like car crashes,
books that change us, neighborhoods
we move into and come to love.
Tristan und Isolde is scarcely the story,
women at least should know the difference
between love and death. No poison cup,
no penance. Merely a notion that the tape-recorder
should have caught some ghost of us: that tape-recorder
not merely played but should have listened to us,
and could instruct those after us:
this we were, this is how we tried to love,
and these are the forces they had ranged against us,
and these are the forces we had ranged within us,
within us and against us, against us and within us.

XVIII

Rain on the West Side Highway,
red light at Riverside:
the more I live the more I think
two people together is a miracle.
You're telling the story of your life
for once, a tremor breaks the surface of your words.
The story of our lives becomes our lives.
Now you're in fugue across what some I'm sure
Victorian poet called the *salt estranging sea.*
Those are the words that come to mind.
I feel estrangement, yes. As I've felt dawn
pushing toward daybreak. Something: a cleft of light——?
Close between grief and anger, a space opens
where I am Adrienne alone. And growing colder.

XIX

Can it be growing colder when I begin
to touch myself again, adhesions pull away?
When slowly the naked face turns from staring backward
and looks into the present,
the eye of winter, city, anger, poverty, and death
and the lips part and say: *I mean to go on living?*
Am I speaking coldly when I tell you in a dream
or in this poem, *There are no miracles?*
(I told you from the first I wanted daily life,
this island of Manhattan was island enough for me.)
If I could let you know—
two women together is a work
nothing in civilization has made simple,
two people together is a work
heroic in its ordinariness,

the slow-picked, halting traverse of a pitch
where the fiercest attention becomes routine
—look at the faces of those who have chosen it.

XX

That conversation we were always on the edge
of having, runs on in my head,
at night the Hudson trembles in New Jersey light
polluted water yet reflecting even
sometimes the moon
and I discern a woman
I loved, drowning in secrets, fear wound round her throat
and choking her like hair. And this is she
with whom I tried to speak, whose hurt, expressive head
turning aside from pain, is dragged down deeper
where it cannot hear me,
and soon I shall know I was talking to my own soul.

XXI

The dark lintels, the blue and foreign stones
of the great round rippled by stone implements
the midsummer night light rising from beneath
the horizon—when I said "a cleft of light"
I meant this. And this is not Stonehenge
simply nor any place but the mind
casting back to where her solitude,
shared, could be chosen without loneliness,
not easily nor without pains to stake out
the circle, the heavy shadows, the great light.
I choose to be a figure in that light,
half-blotted by darkness, something moving

across that space, the color of stone
greeting the moon, yet more than stone
a woman. I choose to walk here. And to draw this circle.

1974–1976

A WOMAN DEAD IN HER FORTIES

1.

Your breasts/   sliced-off   The scars
dimmed   as they would have to be
years later

All the women I grew up with are sitting
half-naked on rocks   in sun
we look at each other and
are not ashamed

and you too have taken off your blouse
but this was not what you wanted:

to show your scarred, deleted torso

I barely glance at you
as if my look could scald you
though I'm the one who loved you

I want to touch my fingers
to where your breasts had been
but we never did such things

You hadn't thought everyone
would look so perfect
unmutilated

you pull on
your blouse again: stern statement:

*There are things I will not share
with everyone*

2.

You send me back to share
my own scars   first of all
with myself

What did I hide from her
what have I denied her
what losses suffered

how in this ignorant body
did she hide

waiting for her release
till uncontrollable light began to pour

from every wound and suture
and all the sacred openings

3.

Wartime.   We sit on warm
weathered, softening grey boards

the ladder glimmers where you told me
the leeches swim

I smell the flame
of kerosene   the pine

boards where we sleep side by side
in narrow cots

the night-meadow exhaling
its darkness   calling

child into woman
child into woman
woman

4.

Most of our love from the age of nine
took the form of jokes and mute

loyalty: you fought a girl
who said she'd knock me down

we did each other's homework
wrote letters   kept in touch, untouching

lied about our lives: I wearing
the face of the proper marriage

you the face of the independent woman
We cleaved to each other across that space

fingering webs
of love and estrangement   till the day

the gynecologist touched your breast
and found a palpable hardness

5.

You played heroic, necessary
games with death

since in your neo-protestant tribe the void
was supposed not to exist

except as a fashionable concept
you had no traffic with

I wish you were here tonight   I want
to yell at you

Don't accept
Don't give in

But would I be meaning your brave
irreproachable life, you dean of women, or

your unfair, unfashionable, unforgivable
woman's death?

6.

You are every woman I ever loved
and disavowed

a bloody incandescent chord strung out
across years, tracts of space

How can I reconcile this passion
with our modesty

your Calvinist heritage
my girlhood frozen into forms

how can I go on this mission
without you

you, who might have told me
everything you feel is true?

7.

Time after time in dreams you rise
reproachful

once from a wheelchair pushed by your father
across a lethal expressway

Of all my dead it's you
who come to me unfinished

You left me amber beads
Strung with turquoise from an Egyptian grave

I wear them wondering
How am I true to you?

I'm half-afraid to write poetry
for you   who never read it much

and I'm left laboring
with the secrets and the silence

In plain language: I never told you how I loved you
we never talked at your deathbed of your death

8.

One autumn evening in a train
catching the diamond-flash of sunset

in puddles along the Hudson
I thought: *I understand*

life and death now, the choices
I didn't know your choice

or how by then you had no choice
how the body tells the truth in its rush of cells

Most of our love took the form
of mute loyalty

we never spoke at your deathbed of your death

but from here on
I want more crazy mourning, more howl, more keening

We stayed mute and disloyal
because we were afraid

I would have touched my fingers
to where your breasts had been
but we never did such things

1974–1977

from NATURAL RESOURCES

4.

Could you imagine a world of women only,
the interviewer asked. *Can you imagine*

a world where women are absent. (He believed
he was joking.) Yet I have to imagine

at one and the same moment, both. Because
I live in both. *Can you imagine,*

the interviewer asked, *a world of men?*
(He thought he was joking.) *If so, then,*

a world where men are absent?
Absently, wearily, I answered: Yes.

5.

The phantom of the man-who-would-understand,
the lost brother, the twin—

for him did we leave our mothers,
deny our sisters, over and over?

did we invent him, conjure him
over the charring log,

nights, late, in the snowbound cabin
did we dream or scry his face

in the liquid embers,
the man-who-would-dare-to-know-us?

6.

It was never the rapist:
it was the brother, lost,

the comrade/twin whose palm
would bear a lifeline like our own:

decisive, arrowy,
forked-lightning of insatiate desire

It was never the crude pestle, the blind
ramrod we were after:

merely a fellow-creature
with natural resources equal to our own

13.

There are words I cannot choose again:
humanism   androgyny

Such words have no shame in them, no diffidence
before the raging stoic grandmothers:

their glint is too shallow, like a dye
that does not permeate

the fibers of actual life
as we live it, now:

this fraying blanket with its ancient stains
we pull across the sick child's shoulder

or wrap around the senseless legs
of the hero trained to kill

this weaving, ragged because incomplete
we turn our hands to, interrupted

over and over, handed down
unfinished, found in the drawer

of an old dresser in the barn,
her vanished pride and care

still urging us, urging on
our works, to close the gap

in the Great Nebula
to help the earth deliver.

14.

The women who first knew themselves
miners, are dead. The rainbow flies

like a flying buttress from the walls
of cloud, the silver-and-green vein

awaits the battering of the pick
the dark lode weeps for light

My heart is moved by all I cannot save:
so much has been destroyed

I have to cast my lot with those
who age after age, perversely,

with no extraordinary power,
reconstitute the world.

1977

TRANSCENDENTAL ETUDE
For Michelle Cliff

This August evening I've been driving
over backroads fringed with queen anne's lace
my car startling young deer in meadows—one
gave a hoarse intake of her breath and all
four fawns sprang after her
into the dark maples.
Three months from today they'll be fair game
for the hit-and-run hunters, glorying
in a weekend's destructive power.
triggers fingered by drunken gunmen, sometimes
so inept as to leave the shattered animal
stunned in her blood. But this evening deep in summer
the deer are still alive and free,
nibbling apples from early-laden boughs
so weighted, so englobed
with already yellowing fruit
they seem eternal, Hesperidean
in the clear-tuned, cricket-throbbing air.

Later I stood in the dooryard,
my nerves singing the immense

fragility of all this sweetness,
this green world already sentimentalized, photographed,
advertised to death. Yet, it persists
stubbornly beyond the fake Vermont
of antique barnboards glazed into discothèques,
artificial snow, the sick Vermont of children
conceived in apathy, grown to winters
of rotgut violence,
poverty gnashing its teeth like a blind cat at their lives.
Still, it persists. Turning off onto a dirt road
from the raw cuts bulldozed through a quiet village
for the tourist run to Canada,
I've sat on a stone fence above a great, soft, sloping field
of musing heifers, a farmstead
slanting its planes calmly in the calm light,
a dead elm raising bleached arms
above a green so dense with life,
minute, momentary life—slugs, moles, pheasants, gnats,
spiders, moths, hummingbirds, groundhogs, butterflies—
a lifetime is too narrow
to understand it all, beginning with the huge
rockshelves that underlie all that life.

No one ever told us we had to study our lives,
make of our lives a study, as if learning natural history
or music, that we should begin
with the simple exercises first
and slowly go on trying
the hard ones, practicing till strength
and accuracy became one with the daring
to leap into transcendence, take the chance
of breaking down in the wild arpeggio
or faulting the full sentence of the fugue.
—And in fact we can't live like that: we take on
everything at once before we've even begun

to read or mark time, we're forced to begin
in the midst of the hardest movement,
the one already sounding as we are born.
At most we're allowed a few months
of simply listening to the simple line
of a woman's voice singing a child
against her heart. Everything else is too soon,
too sudden, the wrenching-apart, that woman's heartbeat
heard ever after from a distance,
the loss of that ground-note echoing
whenever we are happy, or in despair.

Everything else seems beyond us,
we aren't ready for it, nothing that was said
is true for us, caught naked in the argument,
the counterpoint, trying to sightread
what our fingers can't keep up with, learn by heart
what we can't even read. And yet
it *is* this we were born to. We aren't virtuosi
or child prodigies, there are no prodigies
in this realm, only a half-blind, stubborn
cleaving to the timbre, the tones of what we are
—even when all the texts describe it differently.

And we're not performers, like Liszt, competing
against the world for speed and brilliance
(the 79-year-old pianist said, when I asked her
What makes a virtuoso?—Competitiveness.)
The longer I live the more I mistrust
theatricality, the false glamour cast
by performance, the more I know its poverty beside
the truths we are salvaging from
the splitting-open of our lives.
The woman who sits watching, listening,
eyes moving in the darkness

is rehearsing in her body, hearing-out in her blood
a score touched off in her perhaps
by some words, a few chords, from the stage:
a tale only she can tell.

But there come times—perhaps this is one of them—
when we have to take ourselves more seriously or die;
when we have to pull back from the incantations,
rhythms we've moved to thoughtlessly,
and disenthrall ourselves, bestow
ourselves to silence, or a deeper listening, cleansed
of oratory, formulas, choruses, laments, static
crowding the wires. We cut the wires,
find ourselves in free-fall, as if
our true home were the undimensional
solitudes, the rift
in the Great Nebula.
No one who survives to speak
new language, has avoided this:
the cutting-away of an old force that held her
rooted to an old ground
the pitch of utter loneliness
where she herself and all creation
seem equally dispersed, weightless, her being a cry
to which no echo comes or can ever come.

But in fact we were always like this,
rootless, dismembered: knowing it makes the difference.
Birth stripped our birthright from us,
tore us from a woman, from women, from ourselves
so early on
and the whole chorus throbbing at our ears
like midges, told us nothing, nothing
of origins, nothing we needed
to know, nothing that could re-member us.

Only: that it is unnatural,
the homesickness for a woman, for ourselves,
for that acute joy at the shadow her head and arms
cast on a wall, her heavy or slender
thighs on which we lay, flesh against flesh,
eyes steady on the face of love; smell of her milk, her sweat,
terror of her disappearance, all fused in this hunger
for the element they have called most dangerous, to be
lifted breathtaken on her breast, to rock within her
—even if beaten back, stranded again, to apprehend
in a sudden brine-clear thought
trembling like the tiny, orbed, endangered
egg-sac of a new world:
This is what she was to me, and this
is how I can love myself—
as only a woman can love me.

Homesick for myself, for her—as, after the heatwave
breaks, the clear tones of the world
manifest: cloud, bough, wall, insect, the very soul of light:
homesick as the fluted vault of desire
articulates itself: *I am the lover and the loved,*
home and wanderer, she who splits
firewood and she who knocks, a stranger
in the storm, two women, eye to eye
measuring each other's spirit, each other's
limitless desire,
                    a whole new poetry beginning here.

Vision begins to happen in such a life
as if a woman quietly walked away
from the argument and jargon in a room
and sitting down in the kitchen, began turning in her lap
bits of yarn, calico and velvet scraps,
laying them out absently on the scrubbed boards

in the lamplight, with small rainbow-colored shells
sent in cotton-wool from somewhere far away,
and skeins of milkweed from the nearest meadow—
original domestic silk, the finest findings—
and the darkblue petal of the petunia,
and the dry darkbrown lace of seaweed;
not forgotten either, the shed silver
whisker of the cat,
the spiral of paper-wasp-nest curling
beside the finch's yellow feather.
Such a composition has nothing to do with eternity,
the striving for greatness, brilliance—
only with the musing of a mind
one with her body, experienced fingers quietly pushing
dark against bright, silk against roughness,
pulling the tenets of a life together
with no mere will to mastery,
only care for the many-lived, unending
forms in which she finds herself,
becoming now the sherd of broken glass
slicing light in a corner, dangerous
to flesh, now the plentiful, soft leaf
that wrapped round the throbbing finger, soothes the wound;
and now the stone foundation, rockshelf further
forming underneath everything that grows.

1977

from

A WILD
PATIENCE
HAS TAKEN
ME THIS FAR

(1981)

INTEGRITY

the quality or state of being complete: unbroken condition: entirety

—*Webster's*

A wild patience has taken me this far

as if I had to bring to shore
a boat with a spasmodic outboard motor
old sweaters, nets, spray-mottled books
tossed in the prow
some kind of sun burning my shoulder-blades.
Splashing the oarlocks. Burning through.
Your fore-arms can get scalded, licked with pain
in a sun blotted like unspoken anger
behind a casual mist.

The length of daylight
this far north, in this
forty-ninth year of my life
is critical.

The light is critical: of me, of this
long-dreamed, involuntary landing
on the arm of an inland sea.
The glitter of the shoal
depleting into shadow
I recognize: the stand of pines
violet-black really, green in the old postcard
but really I have nothing but myself
to go by; nothing
stands in the realm of pure necessity
except what my hands can hold.

Nothing but myself? ... *My selves.*
After so long, this answer.

As if I had always known
I steer the boat in, simply.
The motor dying on the pebbles
cicadas taking up the hum
dropped in the silence.

Anger and tenderness: my selves.
And now I can believe they breathe in me
as angels, not polarities.
Anger and tenderness: the spider's genius
to spin and weave in the same action
from her own body, anywhere—
even from a broken web.

The cabin in the stand of pines
is still for sale. I know this. Know the print
of the last foot, the hand that slammed and locked that door,
then stopped to wreathe the rain-smashed clematis
back on the trellis
for no one's sake except its own.
I know the chart nailed to the wallboards
the icy kettle squatting on the burner.
The hands that hammered in those nails
emptied that kettle one last time
are these two hands
and they have caught the baby leaping
from between trembling legs
and they have worked the vacuum aspirator
and stroked the sweated temples
and steered the boat here through this hot
misblotted sunlight, critical light
imperceptibly scalding
the skin these hands will also salve.

1978

196

TRANSIT

When I meet the skier she is always
walking, skis and poles shouldered, toward the mountain
free-swinging in worn boots
over the path new-sifted with fresh snow
her greying dark hair almost hidden by
a cap of many colors
her fifty-year-old, strong, impatient body
dressed for cold and speed
her eyes level with mine

And when we pass each other I look into her face
wondering what we have in common
where our minds converge
for we do not pass each other, she passes me
as I halt beside the fence tangled in snow,
she passes me as I shall never pass her
in this life

Yet I remember us together
climbing Chocorua, summer nineteen-forty-five
details of vegetation beyond the timberline
lichens, wildflowers, birds,
amazement when the trail broke out onto the granite ledge
sloped over blue lakes, green pines, giddy air
like dreams of flying

When sisters separate they haunt each other
as she, who I might once have been, haunts me
or is it I who do the haunting
halting and watching on the path
how she appears again through lightly-blowing
crystals, how her strong knees carry her,
how unaware she is, how simple

this is for her, how without let or hindrance
she travels in her body
until the point of passing, where the skier
and the cripple must decide
to recognize each other?

1979

FOR MEMORY

Old words: *trust fidelity*
Nothing new yet to take their place.

I rake leaves, clear the lawn, October grass
painfully green beneath the gold
and in this silent labor thoughts of you
start up
I hear your voice: *disloyalty betrayal*
stinging the wires

I stuff the old leaves into sacks
and still they fall and still
I see my work undone

One shivering rainswept afternoon
and the whole job to be done over

I can't know what you know
unless you tell me
there are gashes in our understandings
of this world
We came together in a common

fury of direction
barely mentioning difference
(what drew our finest hairs
to fire
the deep, difficult troughs
unvoiced)
I fell through a basement railing
the first day of school and cut my forehead open—
did I ever tell you? More than forty years

and I still remember smelling my own blood
like the smell of a new schoolbook

And did you ever tell me
how your mother called you in from play
and from whom? To what? These atoms filmed by ordinary dust
that common life we each and all bent out of orbit from
to which we must return simply to say
this is where I came from
this is what I knew

The past is not a husk   yet change goes on

Freedom. It isn't once, to walk out
under the Milky Way, feeling the rivers
of light, the fields of dark—
freedom is daily, prose-bound, routine
remembering. Putting together, inch by inch
the starry worlds. From all the lost collections.

1979

FOR ETHEL ROSENBERG

convicted, with her husband, of "conspiracy to commit espionage": killed
in the electric chair June 19, 1953

1.

Europe 1953:
throughout my random sleepwalk
the words

scratched on walls, on pavements
painted over railway arches
Liberez les Rosenberg!

Escaping from home I found
home everywhere:
the Jewish question, Communism

marriage itself
a question of loyalty
or punishment

my Jewish father writing me
letters of seventeen pages
finely inscribed harangues

questions of loyalty
and punishment
One week before my wedding

that couple gets the chair
the volts grapple her, don't
kill her fast enough

Liberez les Rosenberg!
I hadn't realized
our family arguments were so important

my narrow understanding
of crime   of punishment
no language for this torment

mystery of that marriage
always both faces
on every front page in the world

Something so shocking   so
unfathomable
it must be pushed aside

2.

She sank however into my soul   A weight of sadness
I hardly can register how deep
her memory has sunk   that wife and mother

like so many
who seemed to get nothing out of any of it
except her children

that daughter   of a family
like so many
needing its female monster

she, actually wishing to be *an artist*
wanting out of poverty
possibly also really wanting
                              revolution

that woman   strapped in the chair
no fear and no regrets
charged by posterity

not with selling secrets to the Communists
but with wanting   *to distinguish*
herself   being a bad daughter   a bad mother

And I   walking to my wedding
by the same token a bad daughter   a bad sister
my forces focussed

on that hardly revolutionary effort
Her life and death   the possible
ranges of disloyalty

so painful   so unfathomable
they must be pushed aside
ignored for years

3.

Her mother testifies against her
Her brother testifies against her
After her death

she becomes a natural prey for pornographers
her death itself a scene
her body *sizzling   half-strapped   whipped like a sail*

She becomes the extremest victim
described nonetheless as *rigid of will*
what are her politics by then   no one knows

Her figure sinks into my soul
a drowned statue
sealed in lead

For years it has lain there   unabsorbed
first as part of that dead couple
on the front pages of the world   the week

I gave myself in marriage
then slowly severing   drifting apart
a separate death   a life unto itself

no longer *the Rosenbergs*
no longer the chosen scapegoat
the family monster

till I hear how she sang
a prostitute to sleep
in the Women's House of Detention

Ethel Greenglass Rosenberg   would you
have marched to take back the night
collected signatures

for battered women who kill
What would you have to tell us
would you have burst the net

4.

Why do I even want to call her up
to console my pain   (she feels no pain at all)
why do I wish to put such questions

to ease myself   (she feels no pain at all
she   finally burned to death   like so many)
why all this exercise of hindsight?

since   if I imagine her at all
I have to imagine first
the pain inflicted on her   by women

her mother testifies against her
her sister-in-law testifies against her
and how she sees it

not the impersonal forces
not the historical reasons
why they might have hated her strength

If I have held her at arm's length till now
if I have still believed it was
my loyalty, my punishment at stake

if I dare imagine her surviving
I must be fair to what she must have lived through
I must allow her to be at last

political in her ways   not in mine
her urgencies perhaps   impervious to mine
defining revolution as she defines it

or, bored to the marrow of her bones
with "politics"
bored with the vast boredom of long pain

small; tiny in fact; in her late sixties
liking her room   her private life
living alone perhaps

no one you could interview
maybe filling a notebook herself
with secrets she has never sold

1980

from THE SPIRIT OF PLACE
For Michelle Cliff

III.

Strangers are an endangered species

In Emily Dickinson's house in Amherst
cocktails are served   the scholars
gather in celebration
their pious or clinical legends
festoon the walls like imitations
of period patterns

     (*. . . and, as I feared, my "life" was made a "victim"*)

The remnants pawed   the relics
the cult assembled in the bedroom
and you   whose teeth were set on edge by churches
resist your shrine

              escape

                  are found

nowhere

        unless in words

                (your own)

All we are strangers—dear—The world is not
acquainted with us, because we are not acquainted
with her. And Pilgrims!—Do you hesitate? and
Soldiers oft—some of us victors, but those I do
not see tonight owing to the smoke.—We are hungry,
and thirsty, sometimes—We are barefoot—and cold—

This place is large enough for both of us
the river-fog will do for privacy
this is my third and last address to you

with the hands of a daughter I would cover you
from all intrusion   even my own
saying   rest to your ghost

with the hands of a sister I would leave your hands
open or closed as they prefer to lie
and ask no more of who or why or wherefore

with the hands of a mother I would close the door
on the rooms you've left behind
and silently pick up my fallen work

V.

Orion plunges like a drunken hunter
over the Mohawk Trail   a parallelogram
slashed with two cuts of steel

A night so clear that every constellation
stands out from an undifferentiated cloud
of stars, a kind of aura

All the figures up there look violent to me
as a pogrom on Christmas Eve in some old country
I want our own earth   not the satellites, our

world as it is   if not as it might be
then as it is: male dominion, gangrape, lynching, pogrom
the Mohawk wraiths in their tracts of leafless birch

watching: will we do better?
The tests I need to pass are prescribed by the spirits
of place   who understand travel but not amnesia

The world as it is: not as her users boast
damaged beyond reclamation by their using
Ourselves as we are   in these painful motions

of staying cognizant: some part of us always
out beyond ourselves
knowing   knowing   knowing

Are we all in training for something we don't name?
to exact reparation for things
done long ago to us and to those who did not

survive what was done to them   whom we ought to honor
with grief   with fury   with action
On a pure night   on a night when pollution

seems absurdity when the undamaged planet seems to turn
like a bowl of crystal in black ether
they are the piece of us that lies out there
knowing   knowing   knowing

1980

from

YOUR NATIVE
LAND,
YOUR LIFE

(1986)

SOURCES

For Helen Smelser
—since 1949—

I

Sixteen years.   The narrow, rough-gullied backroads
almost the same.   The farms: almost the same,
a new barn here, a new roof there, a rusting car,
collapsed sugar-house, trailer, new young wife
trying to make a lawn instead of a dooryard,
new names, old kinds of names: Rocquette, Desmarais,
Clark, Pierce, Stone.   Gossier.   No names of mine.

The vixen I met at twilight on Route 5
south of Willoughby: long dead.   She was an omen
to me, surviving, herding her cubs
in the silvery bend of the road
in nineteen sixty-five.

Shapes of things: so much the same
they feel like eternal forms: the house and barn
on the rise above May Pond; the brow of Pisgah;
the face of milkweed blooming,
brookwater pleating over slanted granite,
boletus under pine, the half-composted needles
it broke through patterned on its skin.
Shape of queen anne's lace, with the drop of blood.
Bladder-campion veined with purple.
Multifoliate heal-all.

II

I refuse to become a seeker for cures.
Everything that has ever
helped me has come through what already
lay stored in me.   Old things, diffuse, unnamed, lie strong
across my heart.
                          This is from where
my strength comes, even when I miss my strength
even when it turns on me
like a violent master.

III

From where?   the voice asks coldly.

This is the voice in cold morning air
that pierces dreams.   *From where does your strength come?*

Old things . . .
                    From where does your strength come, you Southern Jew?
split at the root, raised in a castle of air?

Yes.   I expected this.   I have known for years
the question was coming.   *From where*

(not from these, surely,
Protestant separatists, Jew-baiters, nightriders

who fired in Irasburg in nineteen-sixty-eight
on a black family newly settled in these hills)
                                        From where

the dew grows thick late August on the fierce green grass
and on the wooden sill and on the stone

the mountains stand in an extraordinary
point of no return   though still are green

collapsed shed-boards gleam like pewter in the dew
the realms of touch-me-not   fiery with tiny tongues

cover the wild ground of the woods

IV

With whom do you believe your lot is cast?
From where does your strength come?

I think somehow, somewhere
every poem of mine must repeat those questions

which are not the same.   There is a *whom,* a *where*
that is not chosen   that is given   and sometimes falsely given

in the beginning we grasp whatever we can
to survive

V

All during World War II
I told myself I had some special destiny:
there had to be a reason
I was not living in a bombed-out house
or cellar   hiding out with rats

there had to be a reason
I was growing up safe, American
with sugar rationed in a Mason jar

split at the root   white-skinned social Christian
neither gentile nor Jew

through the immense silence
of the Holocaust

I had no idea of what I had been spared

still less of the women and men   my kin
the Jews of Vicksburg or Birmingham
whose lives must have been strategies no less
than the vixen's on Route 5

VI

If they had played the flute, or chess
I was told   I was not told what they told
their children when the Klan rode
how they might have seen themselves
                              a chosen people

of shopkeepers
clinging by strategy to a way of life
that had its own uses for them

proud of their length of sojourn in America
deploring the late-comers   the peasants from Russia

I saw my father building
his rootless ideology

his private castle in air

in that most dangerous place, the family home
we were the chosen people

In the beginning we grasp whatever we can

VII

For years I struggled with you: your categories, your theories,
your will, the cruelty which came inextricable from your love.   For
years all arguments I carried on in my head were with you.   I saw
myself, the eldest daughter raised as a son, taught to study but not to
pray, taught to hold reading and writing sacred: the eldest daughter
in a house with no son, she who must overthrow the father, take what
he taught her and use it against him.   All this in a castle of air, the
floating world of the assimilated who know and deny they will always
be aliens.

After your death I met you again as the face of patriarchy, could
name at last precisely the principle you embodied, there was an ide-
ology at last which let me dispose of you, identify the suffering you
caused, hate you righteously as part of a system, the kingdom of the
fathers.   I saw the power and arrogance of the male as your true
watermark; I did not see beneath it the suffering of the Jew, the alien
stamp you bore, because you had deliberately arranged that it should
be invisible to me.   It is only now, under a powerful, womanly lens,
that I can decipher your suffering and deny no part of my own.

VIII

Back there in Maryland the stars
showed liquescent, diffuse

in the breathless summer nights
the constellation melted

I thought I was leaving a place of enervation
heading north where the Drinking Gourd

stood cold and steady at last
pointing the way

I thought I was following a track of freedom
and for awhile it was

IX

Why has my imagination stayed
northeast with the ones who stayed

Are there spirits in me, diaspora-driven
that wanted to lodge somewhere

hooked into the "New" Englanders who hung on
here in this stringent space

believing their Biblical language
their harping on righteousness?

And, myself apart, what was this like for them,
this unlikely growing season

after each winter so mean, so mean
the trying-down of the spirit

and the endless rocks in the soil, the endless
purifications of self

there being no distance, no space around
to experiment with life?

X

These upland farms are the farms
of invaders, these villages

white with rectitude and death
are built on stolen ground

The persecuted, pale with anger
know how to persecute

those who feel destined, under god's eye
need never ponder difference

and if they kill others for being who they are
or where they are

is this a law of history
or simply, *what must change?*

XI

If I try to conjure their lives
—who are not my people by any definition—

Yankee Puritans, Québec Catholics
mingled within sight of the Northern Lights

I am forced to conjure a passion
like the tropism in certain plants

bred of a natural region's
repetitive events

beyond the numb of poverty
christian hypocrisy, isolation

—a passion so unexpected
there is no name for it

so quick, fierce, unconditional
short growing season is no explanation.

XII

And has any of this to do with how
Mohawk or Wampanoag knew it?

is the passion I connect with in this air
trace of the original

existences that knew this place
is the region still trying to speak with them

is this light a language
the shudder of this aspen-grove a way

of sending messages
the white mind barely intercepts

are signals also coming back
from the vast diaspora

of the people who kept their promises
as a way of life?

XIII

Coming back after sixteen years
I stare anew at things

that steeple pure and righteous
that clapboard farmhouse

seeing what I hadn't seen before
through barnboards, crumbling plaster

decades of old wallpaper roses
clinging to certain studs

—into that dangerous place
the family home:

There are verbal brutalities
borne thereafter like any burn or scar

there are words pulled down from the walls
like dogwhips

the child backed silent against the wall
trying to keep her eyes dry;   haughty;   in panic

I will never let you know
I will never
let you know

XIV

And if my look becomes the bomb that rips
the family home apart

is this betrayal, that the walls
slice off, the staircase shows

torn-away above the street
that the closets where the clothes hung

hang naked, the room the old
grandmother had to sleep in

the toilet on the landing
the room with the books

where the father walks up and down
telling the child to *work, work*

harder than anyone has worked before?
—But I can't stop seeing like this

more and more I see like this everywhere.

XV

It's an oldfashioned, an outrageous thing
to believe one has a "destiny"

—a thought often peculiar to those
who possess privilege—

but there is something else: the faith
of those despised and endangered

that they are not merely the sum
of damages done to them:

have kept beyond violence the knowledge
arranged in patterns like kente-cloth

unexpected as in batik
recurrent as bitter herbs and unleavened bread

of being a connective link
in a long, continuous way

of ordering hunger, weather, death, desire
and the nearness of chaos.

XVI

The Jews I've felt rooted among
are those who were turned to smoke

Reading of the chimneys against the blear air
I think I have seen them myself

the fog of northern Europe licking its way
along the railroad tracks

to the place where all tracks end
You told me not to look there

to become
a citizen of the world

bound by no tribe or clan
yet dying you followed the Six Day War

with desperate attention
and this summer I lie awake at dawn

sweating the Middle East through my brain
wearing the star of David

on a thin chain at my breastbone

XVII

But there was also the other Jew. The one you most feared, the one from the *shtetl*, from Brooklyn, from the wrong part of history, the wrong accent, the wrong class. The one I left you for.   The one both like and unlike you, who explained you to me for years, who could not explain himself.   The one who said, as if he had memorized the formula, *There's nothing left now but the food and the humor.*   The one who, like you, ended isolate, who had tried to move in the floating world of the assimilated who know and deny they will always be aliens.   Who drove to Vermont in a rented car at dawn and shot himself.   For so many years I had thought you and he were in opposition. I needed your unlikeness then; now it's your likeness that stares me in the face.   There is something more than food, humor, a turn of phrase, a gesture of the hands: there is something more.

XVIII

There is something more than self-hatred. That still outlives
these photos of the old Ashkenazi life:
we are gifted children at camp in the country
or orphaned children in kindergarten
we are hurrying along the rare book dealers' street
with the sunlight striking one side
we are walking the wards of the Jewish hospital
along diagonal squares   young serious nurses
we are part of a family group
formally taken in 1936

222

with tables, armchairs, ferns
(behind us, in our lives, the muddy street
and the ragged shames
the street-musician, the weavers lined for strike)
we are part of a family wearing white head-bandages
we were beaten in a pogrom

The place where all tracks end
is the place where history was meant to stop
but does not stop   where thinking
was meant to stop but does not stop
where the pattern was meant to give way at last

                                    but only

becomes a different pattern
                             terrible, threadbare
strained   familiar on-going

XIX

They say such things are stored
in the genetic code—

half-chances, unresolved
possibilities, the life

passed on because unlived—
a mystic biology?—

I think of the women who sailed to Palestine
years before I was born—

halutzot, pioneers
believing in a new life

socialists, anarchists, jeered
as excitable, sharp of tongue

too filled with life
wanting equality in the promised land

carrying the broken promises
of Zionism in their hearts

along with the broken promises
of communism, anarchism—

makers of miracle who expected miracles
as stubbornly as any housewife does

that the life she gives her life to
shall not be cheap

that the life she gives her life to
shall not turn on her

that the life she gives her life to
shall want an end to suffering

Zion by itself is not enough.

XX

The faithful drudging child
the child at the oak desk whose penmanship,
hard work, style will win her prizes
becomes the woman with a mission, not to win prizes
but to change the laws of history.
How she gets this mission

is not clear, how the boundaries of perfection
explode, leaving her cheekbone grey with smoke
a piece of her hair singed off, her shirt
spattered with earth . . . Say that she grew up in a house
with talk of books, ideal societies—
she is gripped by a blue, a foreign air,
a desert absolute: dragged by the roots of her own will
into another scene of choices.

XXI

YERUSHALAYIM: a vault of golden heat
hard-pulsing from bare stones

the desert's hard-won, delicate green
the diaspora of the stars

thrilling like thousand-year-old locusts
audible yet unheard

a city on a hill
waking with first light to voices

piercing, original, intimate
as if my dreams mixed with the cries

of the oldest, earliest birds
and of all whose wrongs and rights

cry out for explication
as the night pales and one more day

breaks on this *Zion* of hope and fear
and broken promises
                              this promised land

XXII

I have resisted this for years, writing to you as if you could hear
me.   It's been different with my father: he and I always had a
kind of rhetoric going with each other, a battle between us, it didn't
matter if one of us was alive or dead.   But, you, I've had a sense of
protecting your existence, not using it merely as a theme for poetry
or tragic musings; letting you dwell in the minds of those who have
reason to miss you, in your way, or their way, not mine. The living,
writers especially, are terrible projectionists.   I hate the way they
use the dead.

Yet I can't finish this without speaking to you, not simply of
you.   You knew there was more left than food and humor.   Even as
you said that in 1953 I knew it was a formula you had found, to stand
between you and pain.   The deep crevices of black pumpernickel
under the knife, the sweet butter and red onions we ate on those slices;
the lox and cream cheese on fresh onion rolls; bowls of sour cream
mixed with cut radishes, cucumber, scallions; green tomatoes and
kosher dill pickles in half-translucent paper; these, you said, were the
remnants of the culture, along with the fresh *challah* which turned
stale so fast but looked so beautiful.

That's why I want to speak to you now.   To say: no person, try-
ing to take responsibility for her or his identity, should have to be so
alone.   There must be those among whom we can sit down and weep,
and still be counted as warriors.   (I make up this strange, angry
packet for you, threaded with love.)   I think you thought there was
no such place for you, and perhaps there was none then, and perhaps
there is none now; but we will have to make it, we who want an end to
suffering, who want to change the laws of history, if we are not to *give
ourselves away.*

XXIII

Sixteen years ago I sat in this northeast kingdom
reading Gilbert White's *Natural History*
of Selborne   thinking
I can never know this land I walk upon
as that English priest knew his
—a comparable piece of earth—
rockledge   soil   insect   bird   weed   tree

I will never know it so well because . . .

Because you have chosen
something else: to know other things
even the cities which
create of this a myth

Because you grew up in a castle of air
disjunctured

Because without a faith
                    you are faithful

I have wished I could rest among the beautiful and common weeds I
cán name, both here and in other tracts of the globe.   But there is no
finite knowing, no such rest. Innocent birds, deserts, morning-glories,
point to choices, leading away from the familiar. When I speak of an end
to suffering I don't mean anesthesia. I mean knowing the world, and my
place in it, not in order to stare with bitterness or detachment, but as a
powerful and womanly series of choices: and here I write the words,
in their fullness:
powerful;   womanly.

August 1981–
August 1982

NORTH AMERICAN TIME

I

When my dreams showed signs
of becoming
politically correct
no unruly images
escaping beyond borders
when walking in the street I found my
themes cut out for me
knew what I would not report
for fear of enemies' usage
then I began to wonder

II

Everything we write
will be used against us
or against those we love.
These are the terms,
take them or leave them.
Poetry never stood a chance
of standing outside history.
One line typed twenty years ago
can be blazed on a wall in spraypaint
to glorify art as detachment
or torture of those we
did not love but also
did not want to kill

We move   but our words stand
become responsible
for more than we intended

and this is verbal privilege

III

Try sitting at a typewriter
one calm summer evening
at a table by a window
in the country, try pretending
your time does not exist
that you are simply you
that the imagination simply strays
like a great moth, unintentional
try telling yourself
you are not accountable
to the life of your tribe
the breath of your planet

IV

It doesn't matter what you think.
Words are found responsible
all you can do is choose them
or choose
to remain silent.   Or, you never had a choice,
which is why the words that do stand
are responsible

and this is verbal privilege

V

Suppose you want to write
of a woman braiding
another woman's hair—
straight down, or with beads and shells
in three-strand plaits or corn-rows—
you had better know the thickness
the length   the pattern
why she decides to braid her hair
how it is done to her
what country it happens in
what else happens in that country

You have to know these things

VI

Poet, sister: words—
whether we like it or not—
stand in a time of their own.
No use protesting   *I wrote that*
before Kollontai was exiled
Rosa Luxemburg, Malcolm,
Anna Mae Aquash, murdered,
before Treblinka, Birkenau,
Hiroshima, before Sharpeville,
Biafra, Bangladesh, Boston,
Atlanta, Soweto, Beirut, Assam
—those faces, names of places
sheared from the almanac
of North American time

VII

I am thinking this in a country
where words are stolen out of mouths
as bread is stolen out of mouths
where poets don't go to jail
for being poets, but for being
dark-skinned, female, poor.
I am writing this in a time
when anything we write
can be used against those we love
where the context is never given
though we try to explain, over and over
For the sake of poetry at least
I need to know these things

VIII

Sometimes, gliding at night
in a plane over New York City
I have felt like some messenger
called to enter, called to engage
this field of light and darkness.
A grandiose idea, born of flying.
But underneath the grandiose idea
is the thought that what I must engage
after the plane has raged onto the tarmac
after climbing my old stairs, sitting down
at my old window
is meant to break my heart and reduce me to silence.

IX

In North America time stumbles on
without moving, only releasing
a certain North American pain.
Julia de Burgos wrote:
That my grandfather was a slave
is my grief;   had he been a master
that would have been my shame.
A poet's words, hung over a door
in North America, in the year
nineteen-eighty-three.
The almost-full moon rises
timelessly speaking of change
out of the Bronx, the Harlem River
the drowned towns of the Quabbin
the pilfered burial mounds
the toxic swamps, the testing-grounds

and I start to speak again

1983

DREAMS BEFORE WAKING

Despair is the question.

—Elie Wiesel

Hasta tu país cambió. Lo has cambiado tú mismo.

—Nancy Morejón

Despair falls:
the shadow of a building
they are raising in the direct path
of your slender ray of sunlight
Slowly the steel girders grow
the skeletal framework rises
yet the western light still filters
through it all
still glances off the plastic sheeting
they wrap around it
for dead of winter

At the end of winter something changes
a faint subtraction
from consolations you expected
an innocent brilliance that does not come
though the flower shops set out
once again on the pavement
their pots of tight-budded sprays
the bunches of jonquils stiff with cold
and at such a price
though someone must buy them
you study those hues as if with hunger

Despair falls
like the day you come home
from work, a summer evening
transparent with rose-blue light
and see they are filling in

the framework
the girders are rising
beyond your window
that seriously you live
in a different place
though you have never moved

and will not move, not yet
but will give away
your potted plants to a friend
on the other side of town
along with the cut crystal flashing
in the window-frame
will forget the evenings
of watching the street, the sky
the planes in the feathered afterglow:
will learn to feel grateful simply for this foothold

where still you can manage
to go on paying rent
where still you can believe
it's the old neighborhood:
even the woman who sleeps at night
in the barred doorway—wasn't she always there?
and the man glancing, darting
for food in the supermarket trash—
when did his hunger come to this?
what made the difference?
what will make it for you?

What will make it for you?
You don't want to know the stages
and those who go through them don't want to tell
You have your four locks on the door
your savings, your respectable past

your strangely querulous body, suffering
sicknesses of the city no one can name
You have your pride, your bitterness
your memories of sunset
you think you can make it straight through
if you don't speak of despair.

What would it mean to live
in a city whose people were changing
each other's despair into hope?—
You yourself must change it.—
what would it feel like to know
your country was changing?—
You yourself must change it.—
Though your life felt arduous
new and unmapped and strange
what would it mean to stand on the first
page of the end of despair?

1983

UPCOUNTRY

The silver shadow   where the line falls grey
and pearly   the unborn villages quivering
under the rock   the snail   traveling the crevice
the furred, flying white insect like a tiny
intelligence lacing the air
this woman whose lips lie parted
after long speech
her white hair unrestrained

All that you never paid
or have with difficulty paid
attention to

Change and be forgiven!   the roots of the forest
muttered   but you tramped through   guilty
unable to take forgiveness   neither do you
give mercy

She is asleep now   dangerous   her mind
slits the air like silk   travels faster than sound
like scissors flung into the next century

Even as you watch for the trout's hooked stagger
across the lake   the crack of light and the crumpling bear
her mind was on them first

                         when forgiveness ends
her love means danger

1983

POETRY: I

Someone at a table under a brown metal lamp
is studying the history of poetry.
Someone in the library at closing-time
has learned to say *modernism,*
trope, vatic, text.
She is listening for shreds of music.
He is searching for his name
back in the old country.
They cannot learn without teachers.
They are like us   what we were
if you remember.

In a corner of night a voice
Is crying in a kind of whisper:
More!

Can you remember?   when we thought
the poets taught   how to live?
That is not the voice of a critic
nor a common reader
it is someone young   in anger
hardly knowing what to ask
who finds our lines   our glosses
wanting   in this world.

1985

POETRY: III

Even if we knew the children were all asleep
and healthy   the ledgers balanced   the water running
clear in the pipes
                    and all the prisoners free

Even if every word we wrote by then
were honest   the sheer heft
of our living behind it
                    not these sometimes
lax, indolent lines
                    these litanies

Even if we were told   not just by friends
that this was honest work

Even if each of us didn't wear
a brass locket with a picture
of a strangled woman   a girlchild sewn through the crotch

Even if someone had told us, young: *This is not a key*
nor a peacock feather
                    not a kite nor a telephone
This is the kitchen sink   the grinding-stone

would we give ourselves
more calmly over   feel less criminal joy
when the thing comes   as it does come
clarifying grammar
and the fixed and mutable stars—?

1984

YOM KIPPUR 1984

I drew solitude over me, on the lone shore.

—Robinson Jeffers, "Prelude"

For whoever does not afflict his soul throughout this day, shall be
cut off from his people.

—Leviticus 23:29

What is a Jew in solitude?
What would it mean not to feel lonely or afraid
far from your own or those you have called your own?
What is a woman in solitude: a queer woman or man?
In the empty street, on the empty beach, in the desert
what in this world as it is can solitude mean?

The glassy, concrete octagon suspended from the cliffs
with its electric gate, its perfected privacy
is not what I mean
the pick-up with a gun parked at a turn-out in Utah or the Golan
                    Heights
is not what I mean
the poet's tower facing the western ocean, acres of forest planted to
                    the east, the woman reading in the cabin, her
                    attack dog suddenly risen
is not what I mean

Three thousand miles from what I once called home
I open a book searching for some lines I remember
about flowers, something to bind me to this coast as lilacs in the
                    dooryard once
bound me back there—yes, lupines on a burnt mountainside,
something that bloomed and faded and was written down
in the poet's book, forever:

Opening the poet's book
I find the hatred in the poet's heart: . . . *the hateful-eyed*

and human-bodied are all about me: you that love multitude may have
them

Robinson Jeffers, multitude
is the blur flung by distinct forms against these landward valleys
and the farms that run down to the sea; the lupines
are multitude, and the torched poppies, the grey Pacific unrolling
                    its scrolls of surf,
and the separate persons, stooped
over sewing machines in denim dust, bent under the shattering
                    skies of harvest
who sleep by shifts in never-empty beds have their various dreams
Hands that pick, pack, steam, stitch, strip, stuff, shell, scrape,
                    scour, belong to a brain like no other
Must I argue the love of multitude in the blur or defend
a solitude of barbed-wire and searchlights, the survivalist's final
                    solution, have I a choice?

To wander far from your own or those you have called your own
to hear strangeness calling you from far away
and walk in that direction, long and far, not calculating risk
to go to meet the Stranger without fear or weapon, protection
                    nowhere on your mind
(the Jew on the icy, rutted road on Christmas Eve prays for another
                    Jew
the woman in the ungainly twisting shadows of the street: *Make*
                    those be a woman's footsteps; as if she could believe in a
                    woman's god)

Find someone like yourself.   Find others.
Agree you will never desert each other.
Understand that any rift among you
means power to those who want to do you in.

Close to the center, safety; toward the edges, danger.
But I have a nightmare to tell: I am trying to say
that to be with my people is my dearest wish
but that I also love strangers
that I crave separateness
I hear myself stuttering these words
to my worst friends and my best enemies
who watch for my mistakes in grammar
my mistakes in love.
This is the day of atonement; but do my people forgive me?
If a cloud knew loneliness and fear, I would be that cloud.

To love the Stranger, to love solitude—am I writing merely about
                  privilege
about drifting from the center, drawn to edges,
a privilege we can't afford in the world that is,
who are hated as being of our kind: faggot kicked into the icy
                  river, woman dragged from her stalled car
into the mist-struck mountains, used and hacked to death
young scholar shot at the university gates on a summer evening
                  walk, his prizes and studies nothing, nothing
                  availing his Blackness
Jew deluded that she's escaped the tribe, the laws of her exclusion,
                  the men too holy to touch her hand;   Jew who has
                  turned her back
on *midrash* and *mitzvah* (yet wears the *chai* on a thong between her
                  breasts) hiking alone
found with a swastika carved in her back at the foot of the cliffs
                  (did she die as queer or as Jew?)

Solitude, O taboo, endangered species
on the mist-struck spur of the mountain, I want a gun to defend
                  you
In the desert, on the deserted street, I want what I can't have:
your elder sister, Justice, her great peasant's hand outspread

her eye, half-hooded, sharp and true
And I ask myself, have I thrown courage away?

have I traded off something I don't name?
To what extreme will I go to meet the extremist?
What will I do to defend my want or anyone's want to search for
               her spirit-vision
far from the protection of those she has called her own?
Will I find O solitude
your plumes, your breasts, your hair
against my face, as in childhood, your voice like the mockingbird's
singing *Yes, you are loved, why else this song?*
in the old places, anywhere?

What is a Jew in solitude?
What is a woman in solitude, a queer woman or man?
When the winter flood-tides wrench the tower from the rock,
               crumble the prophet's headland, and the farms slide
               into the sea
when leviathan is endangered and Jonah becomes revenger
when center and edges are crushed together, the extremities
               crushed together on which the world was founded
when our souls crash together, Arab and Jew, howling our
               loneliness within the tribes
when the refugee child and the exile's child re-open the blasted and
               forbidden city
when we who refuse to be women and men as women and men are
               chartered, tell our stories of solitude spent in
               multitude
in that world as it may be, newborn and haunted, what will
               solitude mean?

1984–1985

from CONTRADICTIONS: TRACKING POEMS

3.

My mouth hovers across your breasts
in the short grey winter afternoon
in this bed   we are delicate
and tough   so hot with joy we amaze ourselves
tough   and delicate   we play rings
around each other   our daytime candle burns
with its peculiar light   and if the snow
begins to fall outside   filling the branches
and if the night falls   without announcement
these are the pleasures of winter
sudden, wild and delicate   your fingers
exact   my tongue exact at the same moment
stopping to laugh at a joke
my love   hot on your scent   on the cusp of winter

6.

Dear Adrienne:
                          I'm calling you up tonight
as I might call up a friend   as I might call up a ghost
to ask what you intend to do
with the rest of your life.   Sometimes you act
as if you have all the time there is.
I worry about you when I see this.
The prime of life, old age
aren't what they used to be;
making a good death isn't either,
now you can walk around the corner of a wall
and see a light

that already has blown your past away.
Somewhere in Boston   beautiful literature
is being read around the clock
by writers   to signify
their dislike of this.
I hope you've got something in mind.
I hope you have some idea
about the rest of your life.

In sisterhood,

Adrienne

7.

Dear Adrienne,
I feel signified by pain
from my breastbone through my left shoulder down
through my elbow into my wrist is a thread of pain
I am typing this instead of writing by hand
because my wrist on the right side
blooms and rushes with pain
like a neon bulb
You ask me how I'm going to live
the rest of my life
Well, nothing is predictable with pain
Did the old poets write of this?
—in its odd spaces, free,
many have sung and battled—
But I'm already living the rest of my life
not under conditions of my choosing
wired   into pain
rider on the slow train

Yours, Adrienne

15.

You who think I find words for everything,
and you for whom I write this,
how can I show you what I'm barely
coming into possession of, invisible luggage
of more than fifty years, looking at first
glance like everyone else's, turning up
at the airport carousel
and the waiting for it, knowing what nobody
would steal must eventually come round—
feeling obsessed, peculiar, longing?

16.

It's true, these last few years I've lived
watching myself in the act of loss—the art of losing,
Elizabeth Bishop called it, but for me no art
only badly-done exercises
acts of the heart forced to question
its presumptions in this world   its mere excitements
acts of the body forced to measure
all instincts against pain
acts of parting   trying to let go
without giving up   yes   Elizabeth   a city here
a village there   a sister, comrade, cat
and more   no art to this but anger

18.

The problem, unstated till now, is how
to live in a damaged body
in a world where pain is meant to be gagged

uncured   un-grieved-over   The problem is
to connect, without hysteria, the pain
of any one's body with the pain of the body's world
For it is the body's world
they are trying to destroy forever
The best world is the body's world
filled with creatures   filled with dread
misshapen so   yet the best we have
our raft among the abstract worlds
and how I longed to live on this earth
walking her boundaries   never counting the cost

26.

You: air-driven   reft   from the tuber-bitten soil
that was your portion   from the torched-out village
the Marxist study-group   the Zionist cell
café or *cheder*   Zaddik or Freudian   straight or gay
woman or man   O you
stripped   bared   appalled
stretched to mere spirit   yet still physical
your irreplaceable knowledge   lost
at the mud-slick bottom of the world
how you held fast   with your bone-meal fingers
to yourselves   each other   and strangers
how you touched   held-up from falling
what was already half-cadaver
how your life-cry taunted extinction
with its wild, crude   *so what?*
Grief for you has rebellion at its heart
it cannot simply mourn
You: air-driven: reft: are yet our teachers
trying to speak to us in sleep
trying to help us wake

28.

This high summer we love will pour its light
the fields grown rich and ragged in one strong moment
then before we're ready will crash into autumn
with a violence we can't accept
a bounty we can't forgive
Night frost will strike when the noons are warm
the pumpkins wildly glowing   the green tomatoes
straining huge on the vines
queen anne and blackeyed susan will straggle rusty
as the milkweed stakes her claim
she who will stand at last   dark sticks barely rising
up through the snow   her testament of continuation
We'll dream of a longer summer
but this is the one we have:
I lay my sunburnt hand
on your table: this is the time we have

29.

You who think I find words for everything
this is enough for now
cut it short   cut loose from my words

You for whom I write this
in the night hours when the wrecked cartilage
sifts round the mystical jointure of the bones
when the insect of detritus crawls
from shoulder to elbow to wristbone
remember: the body's pain and the pain on the streets
are not the same   but you can learn
from the edges that blur   O you who love clear edges
more than anything   watch the edges that blur

1983–1985

from

TIME'S
POWER

(1989)

SOLFEGGIETTO

1.

Your windfall at fifteen   your Steinway grand
paid for by fire insurance
came to me as birthright   a black cave
with teeth of ebony and ivory
twanging and thundering over the head
of the crawling child   until
that child was set on the big book on the chair
to face the keyboard world of black and white
—already knowing the world was black and white
The child's hands   smaller than a sand-dollar
set on the keys   wired to their mysteries
the child's wits facing the ruled and ruling staves

2.

For years we battled over music lessons
mine, taught by you   Nor did I wonder
what that keyboard meant to you
the hours of solitude   the practising
your life of prize-recitals   lifted hopes
Piatti's nephew praising you at sixteen
scholarships to the North
Or what it was to teach
boarding-school girls what won't be used
shelving ambition   beating time
to "On the Ice at Sweet Briar" or
"The Sunken Cathedral" for a child
counting the minutes and the scales to freedom

3.

Freedom: what could that mean, for you or me?
—Summers of '36, '37, Europe untuned
what I remember isn't lessons
not Bach or Brahms or Mozart
but the rented upright in the summer rental
One Hundred Best-Loved Songs on the piano rack
And so you played, evenings and so we sang
"Steal Away" and "Swanee River,"
"Swing Low," and most of all
"Mine Eyes Have Seen the Glory of the Coming of the Lord"
How we sang out the chorus   how I loved
the watchfires of the hundred circling camps
and *truth is marching on* and *let us die to make men free*

4.

Piano lessons   The mother and the daughter
Their doomed exhaustion   their common mystery
worked out in finger-exercises   Czerny, Hanon
The yellow Schirmer albums   quarter-rests   double-holds
glyphs of an astronomy   the mother cannot teach
the daughter because this is not the story
of a mother teaching magic to her daughter
Side by side I see us locked
My wrists   your voice   are tightened
Passion lives in old songs   in the kitchen
where another woman cooks   teaches   and sings
He shall feed his flock like a shepherd
and in the booklined room
where the Jewish father reads and smokes and teaches
Ecclesiastes, Proverbs, the Song of Songs

The daughter struggles with the strange notations
—dark chart of music's ocean flowers and flags
but would rather learn by ear and heart   The mother
says she must learn to read by sight   not ear and heart

5.

Daughter who fought her mother's lessons—
even today a scrip of music balks me—
I feel illiterate in this
your mother-tongue   Had it been Greek or Slovak
no more could your native alphabet have baffled
your daughter   whom you taught for years
held by a tether   over the ivory
and ebony teeth of the Steinway
                                        It is
the three hundredth anniversary of Johann
Sebastian Bach   My earliest life
woke to his English Suites   under your fingers
I understand a language I can't read
Music you played streams on the car radio
in the freeway night
You kept your passions deep   You have them still
I ask you, both of us
—Did you think mine was a virtuoso's hand?
Did I see power in yours?
What was worth fighting for?   What did you want?
What did I want from you?

1985–1988

DELTA

If you have taken this rubble for my past
raking through it for fragments you could sell
know that I long ago moved on
deeper into the heart of the matter

If you think you can grasp me, think again:
my story flows in more than one direction
a delta springing from the riverbed
with its five fingers spread.

1987

6/21

It's June and summer's height
the longest bridge of light
leaps from all the rivets
of the sky
Yet it's of earth
and nowhere else I have to speak
Only on earth has this light taken on
these swiveled meanings, only on this earth
where we are dying befouled, gritting our teeth
losing our guiding stars
                              has this light
found an alphabet   a mouth

1987

DREAMWOOD

In the old, scratched, cheap wood of the typing stand
there is a landscape, veined, which only a child can see
or the child's older self,
a woman dreaming when she should be typing
the last report of the day.   If this were a map,
she thinks, a map laid down to memorize
because she might be walking it, it shows
ridge upon ridge fading into hazed desert,
here and there a sign of aquifers
and one possible watering-hole.   If this were a map
it would be the map of the last age of her life,
not a map of choices but a map of variations
on the one great choice. It would be the map by which
she could see the end of touristic choices,
of distances blued and purpled by romance,
by which she would recognize that poetry
isn't revolution but a way of knowing
why it must come.   If this cheap, massproduced
wooden stand from the Brooklyn Union Gas Co.,
massproduced yet durable, being here now,
is what it is yet a dream-map
so obdurate, so plain,
she thinks, the material and the dream can join
and that is the poem and that is the late report.

1987

LIVING MEMORY

Open the book of tales you knew by heart,
begin driving the old roads again,
repeating the old sentences, which have changed
minutely from the wordings you remembered.
A full moon on the first of May
drags silver film on the Winooski River.
The villages are shut
for the night, the woods are open
and soon you arrive at a crossroads
where late, late in time you recognize
part of yourself is buried.   Call it Danville,
village of water-witches.

From here on instinct is uncompromised and clear:
the tales come crowding like the Kalevala
longing to burst from the tongue.   Under the trees
of the backroad you rumor the dark
with houses, sheds, the long barn
moored like a barge on the hillside.
Chapter and verse.   A mailbox.   A dooryard.
A drink of springwater from the kitchen tap.
An old bed, old wallpaper.   Falling asleep like a child
in the heart of the story.

Reopen the book.   A light mist soaks the page,
blunt naked buds tip the wild lilac scribbled
at the margin of the road, no one knows when.
Broken stones of drywall mark the onset
of familiar paragraphs slanting up and away
each with its own version, nothing ever
has looked the same from anywhere.

We came like others to a country of farmers—
Puritans, Catholics, Scotch Irish, Québecois:
bought a failed Yankee's empty house and barn
from a prospering Yankee,
Jews following Yankee footprints,
prey to many myths but most of all
that Nature makes us free.   That the land can save us.
Pioneer, indigenous; we were neither.

You whose stories these farms secrete,
you whose absence these fields publish,
all you whose lifelong travail
took as given this place and weather
who did what you could with the means you had—
it was pick and shovel work
done with a pair of horses, a stone boat
a strong back, and an iron bar: clearing pasture—
Your memories crouched, foreshortened in our text.
Pages torn.   New words crowding the old.

I knew a woman whose clavicle was smashed
inside a white clapboard house with an apple tree
and a row of tulips by the door.   I had a friend
with six children and a tumor like a seventh
who drove me to my driver's test and in exchange
wanted to see Goddard College, in Plainfield.   She'd heard
women without diplomas could study there.
I knew a woman who walked
straight across cut stubble in her bare feet away,
women who said, *He's a good man, never*
laid a hand to me as living proof.
A man they said fought death
to keep fire for his wife for one more winter, leave
a woodpile to outlast him.

I was left the legacy of a pile of stovewood
split by a man in the mute chains of rage.
The land he loved as landscape
could not unchain him.   There are many,
Gentile and Jew, it has not saved.   Many hearts have burst
over these rocks, in the shacks
on the failure sides of these hills.   Many guns
turned on brains already splitting
in silence.   Where are those versions?
Written-across like nineteenth-century letters
or secrets penned in vinegar, invisible
till the page is held over flame.

I was left the legacy of three sons
—as if in an old legend of three brothers
where one changes into a rufous hawk
one into a snowy owl
one into a whistling swan
and each flies to the mother's side
as she travels, bringing something she has lost,
and she sees their eyes are the eyes of her children
and speaks their names and they become her sons.
But there is no one legend and one legend only.

This month the land still leafless, out from snow
opens in all directions, the transparent woods
with sugar-house, pond, cellar-hole unscreened.
Winter and summer cover the closed roads
but for a few weeks they lie exposed,
the old nervous-system of the land.   It's the time
when history speaks in a row of crazy fence-poles
a blackened chimney, houseless, a spring
soon to be choked in second growth
a stack of rusting buckets, a rotting sledge.

It's the time when your own living
laid open between seasons
ponders clues like the *One Way* sign defaced
to *Bone Way,* the stones
of a graveyard in Vermont, a Jewish cemetery
in Birmingham, Alabama.
How you have needed these places,
as a tall gaunt woman used to need to sit
at the knees of bronze-hooded *Grief*
by Clover Adams' grave.
But you will end somewhere else, a sift of ashes
awkwardly flung by hands you have held and loved
or, nothing so individual, bones reduced
with, among, other bones, anonymous,
or wherever the Jewish dead
have to be sought in the wild grass overwhelming
the cracked stones. Hebrew spelled in wilderness.

All we can read is life.   Death is invisible.
A yahrzeit candle belongs
to life.   The sugar skulls
eaten on graves for the Day of the Dead
belong to life.   To the living.   The Kaddish is to the living,
the Day of the Dead, for the living.   Only the living
invent these plumes, tombs, mounds, funeral ships,
living hands turn the mirrors to the walls,
tear the boughs of yew to lay on the casket,
rip the clothes of mourning.   Only the living
decide death's color: is it white or black?
The granite bulkhead
incised with names, the quilt of names, were made
by the living, for the living.
                              I have watched
films from a Pathé camera, a picnic
in sepia, I have seen my mother

tossing an acorn into the air;
my grandfather, alone in the heart of his family;
my father, young, dark, theatrical;
myself, a six-month child.
Watching the dead we see them living
their moments, they were at play, nobody thought
they would be watched so.
                              When Selma threw
her husband's ashes into the Hudson
and they blew back on her and on us, her friends,
it was life.   Our blood raced in that gritty wind.

Such details get bunched, packed, stored
in these cellar-holes of memory
so little is needed
to call on the power, though you can't name its name:
It has its ways of coming back:
a truck going into gear on the crown of the road
the white-throat sparrow's notes
the moon in her fullness standing
right over the concrete steps the way
she stood the night they landed there.
                                        From here
nothing has changed, and everything.

The scratched and treasured photograph Richard showed me
taken in '29, the year I was born:
it's the same road I saw
strewn with the Perseids one August night,
looking older, steeper than now
and rougher, yet I knew it.   Time's
power, the only just power—would you
give it away?

1988

260

from

AN ATLAS
OF THE
DIFFICULT
WORLD

(1991)

AN ATLAS OF THE DIFFICULT WORLD

I

A dark woman, head bent, listening for something
—a woman's voice, a man's voice or
voice of the freeway, night after night, metal streaming downcoast
past eucalyptus, cypress, agribusiness empires
THE SALAD BOWL OF THE WORLD, gurr of small planes
dusting the strawberries, each berry picked by a hand
in close communion, strawberry blood on the wrist,
Malathion in the throat, communion,
the hospital at the edge of the fields,
prematures slipping from unsafe wombs,
the labor and delivery nurse on her break watching
planes dusting rows of pickers.
Elsewhere declarations are made: at the sink
rinsing strawberries flocked and gleaming, fresh from market
one says: "On the pond this evening is a light
finer than my mother's handkerchief
received from her mother, hemmed and initialed
by the nuns in Belgium."
One says: "I can lie for hours
reading and listening to music. But sleep comes hard.
I'd rather lie awake and read."   One writes:
"Mosquitoes pour through the cracks
in this cabin's walls, the road
in winter is often impassable,
I live here so I don't have to go out and act,
I'm trying to hold onto my life, it feels like nothing."
One says: "I never knew from one day to the next
where it was coming from: I had to make my life happen
from day to day.   Every day an emergency.

Now I have a house, a job from year to year.
What does that make me?"
In the writing workshop a young man's tears
wet the frugal beard he's grown to go with his poems
hoping they have redemption stored
in their lines, maybe will get him home free.   In the classroom
eight-year-old faces are grey.   The teacher knows which children
have not broken fast that day,
remembers the Black Panthers spooning cereal.

•

I don't want to hear how he beat her after the earthquake,
tore up her writing, threw the kerosene
lantern into her face waiting
like an unbearable mirror of his own.   I don't
want to hear how she finally ran from the trailer
how he tore the keys from her hands, jumped into the truck
and backed it into her.   I don't want to think
how her guesses betrayed her—that he meant well, that she
was really the stronger and ought not to leave him
to his own apparent devastation.   I don't want to know
wreckage, dreck and waste, but these are the materials
and so are the slow lift of the moon's belly
over wreckage, dreck, and waste, wild treefrogs calling in
another season, light and music still pouring over
our fissured, cracked terrain.

•

Within two miles of the Pacific rounding
this long bay, sheening the light for miles
inland, floating its fog through redwood rifts and over
strawberry and artichoke fields, its bottomless mind
returning always to the same rocks, the same cliffs, with
ever-changing words, always the same language
—this is where I live now.   If you had known me

once, you'd still know me now though in a different
light and life.   This is no place you ever knew me.

But it would not surprise you
to find me here, walking in fog, the sweep of the great ocean
eluding me, even the curve of the bay, because as always
I fix on the land.   I am stuck to earth.   What I love here
is old ranches, leaning seaward, lowroofed spreads between rocks
small canyons running through pitched hillsides
liveoaks twisted on steepness, the eucalyptus avenue leading
to the wrecked homestead, the fogwreathed heavy-chested cattle
on their blond hills.   I drive inland over roads
closed in wet weather, past shacks hunched in the canyons
roads that crawl down into darkness and wind into light
where trucks have crashed and riders of horses tangled
to death with lowstruck boughs.   These are not the roads
you knew me by.   But the woman driving, walking, watching
for life and death, is the same.

II

Here is a map of our country:
here is the Sea of Indifference, glazed with salt
This is the haunted river flowing from brow to groin
we dare not taste its water
This is the desert where missiles are planted like corms
This is the breadbasket of foreclosed farms
This is the birthplace of the rockabilly boy
This is the cemetery of the poor
who died for democracy   This is a battlefield
from a nineteenth-century war   the shrine is famous
This is the sea-town of myth and story   when the fishing fleets
went bankrupt   here is where the jobs were   on the pier
processing frozen fishsticks   hourly wages and no shares

These are other battlefields   Centralia   Detroit
here are the forests primeval   the copper   the silver lodes
These are the suburbs of acquiescence   silence rising fumelike
              from the streets
This is the capital of money and dolor whose spires
flare up through air inversions whose bridges are crumbling
whose children are drifting blind alleys pent
between coiled rolls of razor wire
I promised to show you a map you say but this is a mural
then yes let it be   these are small distinctions
where do we see it from is the question

III

Two five-pointed star-shaped glass candleholders, bought at the
              Ben Franklin, Barton, twenty-three years ago, one
              chipped
—now they hold half-burnt darkred candles, and in between
a spider is working, the third point of her filamental passage
a wicker basket-handle.   All afternoon I've sat
at this table in Vermont, reading, writing, cutting an apple in
              slivers
and eating them, but mostly gazing down through the windows
at the long scribble of lake due south
where the wind and weather come from.   There are bottles set in
              the windows
that children dug up in summer woods or bought for nickels and
              dimes
in dark shops that are no more, gold-brown, foam-green or cobalt
              glass, blue that gave way to the cobalt
              bomb.   The woods
are still on the hill behind the difficult unknowable
incommensurable barn.   The wind's been working itself up
in low gusts gnashing the leaves left chattering on branches

or drifting over still-green grass;   but it's been a warm wind.
An autumn without a killing frost so far, still warm
feels like a time of self-deception, a memory of pushing
limits in youth, that intricate losing game of innocence long
                    overdue.
Frost is expected tonight, gardens are gleaned, potplants taken in,
          there is talk of withering, of wintering-over.

•

North of Willoughby the back road to Barton
turns a right-hand corner on a high plateau
bitten by wind now and rimed grey-white
—farms of rust and stripping paint, the shortest growing season
south of Quebec, a place of sheer unpretentious hardship, dark
                    pines stretching away
toward Canada.   There was a one-room schoolhouse
by a brook where we used to picnic, summers, a little world
of clear bubbling water, cowturds, moss, wild mint, wild mush-
          rooms under the pines.
One hot afternoon I sat there reading Gaskell's *Life of Charlotte
          Brontë*—the remote
upland village where snow lay long and late, the deep-rutted
          roads, the dun and grey moorland
—trying to enfigure such a life, how genius
unfurled in the shortlit days, the meagre means of that house. I
          never thought
of lives at that moment around me, what girl dreamed
and was extinguished in the remote back-country I had come to
          love,
reader reading under a summer tree in the landscape
of the rural working poor.

Now the panes are black and from the south the wind still stag-
          gers, creaking the house:
brown milkweeds toss in darkness below but I cannot see them

the room has lost the window and turned into itself: two corner
                    shelves of things
both useful and unused, things arrived here by chance or choice,
                    two teapots, one broken-spouted, red and blue
came to me with some books from my mother's mother, my
                    grandmother Mary
who travelled little, loved the far and strange, bits of India, Asia
and this teapot of hers was Chinese or she thought it was
—the other given by a German Jew, a refugee who killed herself:
Midlands flowered ware, and this too cannot be used because
                    coated inside—why?—with flaking paint:
"You will always use it for flowers," she instructed when she
                    gave it.
In a small frame, under glass, my father's bookplate, engraved in
                    his ardent youth, the cleft tree-trunk and the win-
                    tering ants:
Without labor, no sweetness—motto I breathed in from him and
                    learned in grief and rebellion to take and use
—and later learned that not all labor ends in sweetness.
A little handwrought iron candlestick, given by another German
                    woman
who hidden survived the Russian soldiers beating the walls in
                    1945,
emigrated, married a poet.   I sat many times at their table.
                    They are now long apart.
Some odd glasses for wine or brandy, from an ignorant, passion-
                    ate time—we were in our twenties—
with the father of the children who dug for old medicine bottles
                    in the woods
—afternoons listening to records, reading Karl Shapiro's *Poems
                    of a Jew* and Auden's "In Sickness and in Health"
                    aloud, using the poems to talk to each other
—now it's twenty years since last I heard that intake
of living breath, as if language were too much to bear,
that voice overcast like klezmer with echoes, uneven, edged,

                    torn, Brooklyn street crowding Harvard Yard
—I'd have known any syllable anywhere.

Stepped out onto the night-porch.   That wind has changed,
                    though still from the south
it's blowing up hard now, no longer close to earth but driving
                    high
into the crowns of the maples, into my face
almost slamming the stormdoor into me.   But it's warm, warm,
pneumonia wind, death of innocence wind, unwinding wind,
time-hurtling wind.   And it has a voice in the house.   I hear
conversations that can't be happening, overhead in the bedrooms
and I'm not talking of ghosts.   The ghosts are here of course but
                    they speak plainly
—haven't I offered food and wine, listened well for them all
                    these years,
not only those known in life but those before our time
of self-deception, our intricate losing game of innocence long
                    overdue?

•

The spider's decision is made, her path cast, candle-wick to
                    wicker handle to candle,
in the air, under the lamp, she comes swimming toward me
(have I been sitting here so long?)   she will use everything,
                    nothing comes without labor, she is working so
                    hard and I know
nothing all winter can enter this house or this web, not all labor
                    ends in sweetness.
But how do I know what she needs?   Maybe simply
to spin herself a house within a house, on her own terms
in cold, in silence.

IV

Late summers, early autumns, you can see something that binds
the map of this country together: the girasol, orange gold-
                petalled
with her black eye, laces the roadsides from Vermont to
                California
runs the edges of orchards, chain-link fences
milo fields and malls, schoolyards and reservations
truckstops and quarries, grazing ranges, graveyards
of veterans, graveyards of cars hulked and sunk, her tubers the
                jerusalem artichoke
that has fed the Indians, fed the hobos, could feed us all.
Is there anything in the soil, cross-country, that makes for
a plant so generous?   *Spendthrift* we say, as if
accounting nature's waste.   Ours darkens
the states to their strict borders, flushes
down borderless streams, leaches from lakes to the curdled foam
down by the riverside.

Waste.   Waste.   The watcher's eye put out, hands of the
                builder severed, brain of the maker starved
those who could bind, join, reweave, cohere, replenish
now at risk in this segregate republic
locked away out of sight and hearing, out of mind, shunted aside
those needed to teach, advise, persuade, weigh arguments
those urgently needed for the work of perception
work of the poet, the astronomer, the historian, the architect of
                new streets
work of the speaker who also listens
meticulous delicate work of reaching the heart of the desperate
                woman, the desperate man
—never-to-be-finished, still unbegun work of repair—it cannot
                be done without them
and where are they now?

V

Catch if you can your country's moment, begin
where any calendar's ripped-off: Appomattox
Wounded Knee, Los Alamos, Selma, the last airlift from Saigon
the ex-Army nurse hitch-hiking from the debriefing center; medal
                    of spit on the veteran's shoulder
—catch if you can this unbound land these states without a cause
earth of despoiled graves and grazing these embittered brooks
these pilgrim ants pouring out from the bronze eyes, ears,
                    nostrils,
the mouth of Liberty
                    over the chained bay waters
                                                            San Quentin:
once we lost our way and drove in under the searchlights to the
                    gates
end of visiting hours, women piling into cars
the bleak glare aching over all
                              Where are we moored?   What
                              are the bindings?   What be-
                              hooves us?

Driving the San Francisco–Oakland Bay Bridge
no monument's in sight but fog
prowling Angel Island muffling Alcatraz
poems in Cantonese inscribed on fog
no icon lifts a lamp here
history's breath blotting the air
over Gold Mountain   a transfer
of patterns like the transfer of African appliqué
to rural Alabama   voices alive in legends, curses
tongue-lashings
                    poems on a weary wall
And when light swivels off Angel Island and Alcatraz
when the bays leap into life

                              views of the Palace of Fine Arts,
                              TransAmerica
when sunset bathes the three bridges
                                    still
old ghosts crouch hoarsely whispering
under Gold Mountain

•

North and east of the romantic headlands there are roads into tule
                       fog
places where life is cheap poor quick unmonumented
Rukeyser would have guessed it coming West for the opening
of the great red bridge   *There are roads to take* she wrote
when you think of your country   driving south
to West Virginia Gauley Bridge silicon mines the flakes of it
                        heaped like snow, death-angel white
—poet journalist pioneer mother
uncovering her country: *there are roads to take*

•

I don't want to know how he tracked them
along the Appalachian Trail, hid close
by their tent, pitched as they thought in seclusion
killing one woman, the other
dragging herself into town   his defense they had teased his
                  loathing
of what they were   I don't want to know
but this is not a bad dream of mine   these are the materials
and so are the smell of wild mint and coursing water remembered
and the sweet salt darkred tissue I lay my face
upon, my tongue within.
                  A crosshair against the pupil of an eye
could blow my life from hers
a cell dividing without maps, sliver of ice beneath a wheel
could do the job.   Faithfulness isn't the problem.

VI

A potato explodes in the oven.   Poetry and famine:
the poets who never starved, whose names we know
the famished nameless taking ship with their hoard of poetry
Annie Sullivan half-blind in the workhouse enthralling her child-
                    mates
with lore her father had borne in his head from Limerick along
                    with the dream of work
and *hatred of England smouldering like a turf-fire*. But a poetry older
                    than hatred. Poetry
in the workhouse, laying of the rails, a potato splattering oven
                    walls
poetry of cursing and silence, bitter and deep, shallow and
                    drunken
poetry of priest-talk, of I.R.A.-talk, kitchen-talk, dream-talk,
                    tongues despised
in cities where in a mere fifty years language has rotted to jargon,
                    lingua franca of inclusion
from turns of speech ancient as the potato, muttered at the coals
                    by women and men
rack-rented, harshened, numbed by labor ending
in root-harvest rotted in field. 1847. No relief. No succour.
America. Meat three times a day, they said.   Slaves—You would
                    not be that.

VII (The Dream-Site)

Some rooftop, water-tank looming, street-racket strangely quelled
and others known and unknown there, long sweet summer eve-
                    ning on the tarred roof:
leaned back your head to the nightvault swarming with stars
the Pleiades broken loose, not seven but thousands
every known constellation flinging out fiery threads

and you could distinguish all
—cobwebs, tendrils, anatomies of stars
coherently hammocked, blueblack avenues between
—you knew your way among them, knew you were part of them
until, neck aching, you sat straight up and saw:

It was New York, the dream-site
the lost city the city of dreadful light
where once as the sacks of garbage rose
like barricades around us we
stood listening to riffs from Pharaoh Sanders' window
on the brownstone steps
went striding the avenues in our fiery hair
in our bodies young and ordinary riding the subways reading
or pressed against other bodies
feeling in them the maps of Brooklyn Queens Manhattan
The Bronx unscrolling in the long breakneck
express plunges
                          as darkly we felt our own blood
streaming   a living city overhead
coherently webbed and knotted   bristling
we and all the others
                          known and unknown
living its life

VIII

He thought there would be a limit and that it would stop him.
                    He depended on that:
the cuts would be made by someone else, the direction
come from somewhere else, arrows flashing on the freeway.
That he'd end somewhere gazing
straight into It was what he imagined and nothing beyond.
That he'd end facing as limit a thing without limits and so he

flung

and burned and hacked and bled himself toward that (if I
                understand

this story at all). What he found: FOR SALE: DO NOT
                DISTURB

OCCUPANT on some cliffs;   some ill-marked, ill-kept roads

ending in warnings about shellfish in Vietnamese, Spanish and
                English.

But the spray was any color he could have dreamed

—gold, ash, azure, smoke, moonstone—

and from time to time the ocean swirled up through the eye of a
                rock and taught him

limits.   Throwing itself backward, singing and sucking, no
                teacher, only its violent

self, the Pacific, dialectical waters rearing

their wild calm constructs, momentary, ancient.

•

If your voice could overwhelm those waters, what would it say?

What would it cry of the child swept under, the mother

on the beach then, in her black bathing suit, walking straight
                out

into the glazed lace as if she never noticed, what would it say of
                the father

facing inland in his shoes and socks at the edge of the tide,

what of the lost necklace glittering twisted in foam?

•

If your voice could crack in the wind hold its breath still as the
                rocks

what would it say to the daughter searching the tidelines for a
                bottled message

from the sunken slaveships?   what of the huge sun slowly de-
                faulting into the clouds

what of the picnic stored in the dunes at high tide, full of the

            moon, the basket
with sandwiches, eggs, paper napkins, can-opener, the meal
packed for a family feast, excavated now by scuttling
ants, sandcrabs, dune-rats, because no one understood
all picnics are eaten on the grave?

IX

On this earth, in this life, as I read your story, you're lonely.
Lonely in the bar, on the shore of the coastal river
with your best friend, his wife, and your wife, fishing
lonely in the prairie classroom with all the students who love
            you. You know some ghosts
come everywhere with you yet leave them unaddressed
for years.   You spend weeks in a house
with a drunk, you sober, whom you love, feeling lonely.
You grieve in loneliness, and if I understand you fuck in
            loneliness.

I wonder if this is a white man's madness.
I honor your truth and refuse to leave it at that.

What have I learned from stories of the hunt, of lonely men in
            gangs?
But there were other stories:
one man riding the Mohave Desert
another man walking the Grand Canyon.
I thought those solitary men were happy, as ever they had been.

Indio's long avenues
of Medjool date-palm and lemon sweep to the Salton Sea
in Yucca Flats the high desert reaches higher, bleached and spare
            of talk.
At Twentynine Palms I found the grave
of Maria Eleanor Whallon, eighteen years, dead at the watering-

hole in 1903, under the now fire-branded palms
Her mother traveled on alone to cook in the mining camps.

X

Soledad. = f. *Solitude, loneliness, homesickness; lonely retreat.*
Winter sun in the rosetrees.
An old Mexican with a white moustache prunes them back
        spraying
the cut branches with dormant oil.   The old paper-bag-brown
        adobe walls
stretch apart from the rebuilt mission, in their own time.   It is
        lonely here
in the curve of the road winding through vast brown fields
        machine-engraved in furrows
of relentless precision.   In the small chapel
La Nuestra Señora de la Soledad dwells in her shallow arch
painted on either side with columns.   She is in black lace crisp as
        cinders
from head to foot.   Alone, solitary, homesick
in her lonely retreat.   Outside black olives fall and smash
littering and staining the beaten path.   The gravestones of the
        padres
are weights pressing down on the Indian artisans.   It is the sixth
        day of another war.

•

Across the freeway stands another structure
from the other side of the mirror   *it destroys*
the logical processes of the mind, a man's thoughts
become completely disorganized, madness streaming from every throat
frustrated sounds from the bars, metallic sounds from the walls
the steel trays, iron beds bolted to the wall, the smells, the human waste.
To determine how men will behave once they enter prison
it is of first importance to know that prison.   (From the freeway

gun-turrets planted like water-towers in another garden, out-
                buildings spaced in winter sun
and the concrete mass beyond: who now writes letters deep in-
                side that cave?)

If my instructor tells me that the world and its affairs
are run as well as they possibly can be, that I am governed
by wise and judicious men, that I am free and should be happy,
and if when I leave the instructor's presence and encounter
the exact opposite, if I actually sense or see confusion, war,
recession, depression, death and decay, is it not reasonable
that I should become perplexed?
                                From eighteen to twenty-eight
                                        of his years
a young man schools himself, argues,
debates, trains, lectures to himself,
teaches himself Swahili, Spanish, learns
five new words of English every day,
chainsmokes, reads, writes letters.
In this college of force he wrestles bitterness,
self-hatred, sexual anger, cures his own nature.
Seven of these years in solitary.   Soledad.

But the significant feature of the desperate man reveals itself
when he meets other desperate men, directly or vicariously;
and he experiences his first kindness, someone to strain with him,
to strain to see him as he strains to see himself,
someone to understand, someone to accept the regard,
the love, that desperation forces into hiding.
Those feelings that find no expression in desperate times
store themselves up in great abundance, ripen, strengthen,
and strain the walls of their repository to the utmost;
where the kindred spirit touches this wall it crumbles—
no one responds to kindness, no one is more sensitive to it
than the desperate man.

XI

One night on Monterey Bay the death-freeze of the century:
a precise, detached caliper-grip holds the stars and the quarter-
                    moon
in arrest: the hardiest plants crouch shrunken, a "killing frost"
on bougainvillea, Pride of Madeira, roseate black-purple succu-
                    lents bowed
juices sucked awry in one orgy of freezing
slumped on their stems like old faces evicted from cheap hotels
—*into the streets of the universe, now!*

Earthquake and drought followed by freezing followed by war
Flags are blossoming now where little else is blossoming
and I am bent on fathoming what it means to love my country.
The history of this earth and the bones within it?
Soils and cities, promises made and mocked, plowed contours of
                    shame and of hope?
Loyalties, symbols, murmurs extinguished and echoing?
Grids of states stretching westward, underground waters?
Minerals, traces, rumors I am made from, morsel, minuscule
                    fibre, one woman
like and unlike so many, fooled as to her destiny, the scope of
                    her task?
One citizen like and unlike so many, touched and untouched in
                    passing
—each of us now a driven grain, a nucleus, a city in crisis
some busy constructing enclosures, bunkers, to escape the com-
                    mon fate
some trying to revive dead statues to lead us, breathing their
                    breath against marble lips
some who try to teach the moment, some who preach the
                    moment
some who aggrandize, some who diminish themselves in the face
                    of half-grasped events

—power and powerlessness run amuck, a tape reeling backward
                    in jeering, screeching syllables—
some for whom war is new, others for whom it merely continues
                    the old paroxysms of time
some marching for peace who for twenty years did not march for
                    justice
some for whom peace is a white man's word and a white man's
                    privilege
some who have learned to handle and contemplate the shapes of
                    powerlessness and power
as the nurse learns hip and thigh and weight of the body he has
                    to lift and sponge, day upon day
as she blows with her every skill on the spirit's embers still burn-
                    ing by their own laws in the bed of death.
A patriot is not a weapon.   A patriot is one who wrestles for the
                    soul of her country
as she wrestles for her own being, for the soul of his country
(gazing through the great circle at Window Rock into the sheen
                    of the Viet Nam Wall)
as he wrestles for his own being.   A patriot is a citizen trying to
                    wake
from the burnt-out dream of innocence, the nightmare
of the white general and the Black general posed in their
                    camouflage,
to remember her true country, remember his suffering land:
                    remember
that blessing and cursing are born as twins and separated at birth
to meet again in mourning
that the internal emigrant is the most homesick of all women and
                    of all men
that every flag that flies today is a cry of pain.
                    Where are we moored?
                    What are the bindings?
                    What behooves us?

XII

What homage will be paid to a beauty built to last
from inside out, executing the blueprints of resistance and mercy
drawn up in childhood, in that little girl, round-faced with
                clenched fists, already acquainted with mourning
in the creased snapshot you gave me?   What homage will be
                paid to beauty
that insists on speaking truth, knows the two are not always the
                same,
beauty that won't deny, is itself an eye, will not rest under
                contemplation?
Those low long clouds we were driving under a month ago in
                New Mexico, clouds an arm's reach away
were beautiful and we spoke of it but I didn't speak then
of your beauty at the wheel beside me, dark head steady, eyes
                drinking the spaces
of crimson, indigo, Indian distance, Indian presence,
your spirit's gaze informing your body, impatient to mark what's
                possible, impatient to mark
what's lost, deliberately destroyed, can never any way be
                returned,
your back arched against all icons, simulations, dead letters
your woman's hands turning the wheel or working with shears,
                torque wrench, knives with salt pork, onions, ink
                and fire
your providing sensate hands, your hands of oak and silk, of
                blackberry juice and drums
—I speak of them now.

For M.

XIII (Dedications)

I know you are reading this poem
late, before leaving your office
of the one intense yellow lamp-spot and the darkening window
in the lassitude of a building faded to quiet
long after rush-hour.   I know you are reading this poem
standing up in a bookstore far from the ocean
on a grey day of early spring, faint flakes driven
across the plains' enormous spaces around you.
I know you are reading this poem
in a room where too much has happened for you to bear
where the bedclothes lie in stagnant coils on the bed
and the open valise speaks of flight
but you cannot leave yet.   I know you are reading this poem
as the underground train loses momentum and before running
                    up the stairs
toward a new kind of love
your life has never allowed.
I know you are reading this poem by the light
of the television screen where soundless images jerk and slide
while you wait for the newscast from the *intifada*.
I know you are reading this poem in a waiting-room
of eyes met and unmeeting, of identity with strangers.
I know you are reading this poem by fluorescent light
in the boredom and fatigue of the young who are counted out,
count themselves out, at too early an age.   I know
you are reading this poem through your failing sight, the thick
lens enlarging these letters beyond all meaning yet you read on
because even the alphabet is precious.
I know you are reading this poem as you pace beside the stove
warming milk, a crying child on your shoulder, a book in your
                    hand
because life is short and you too are thirsty.
I know you are reading this poem which is not in your language

guessing at some words while others keep you reading
and I want to know which words they are.
I know you are reading this poem listening for something, torn
                    between bitterness and hope
turning back once again to the task you cannot refuse.
I know you are reading this poem because there is nothing else
                    left to read
there where you have landed, stripped as you are.

1990–1991

from EASTERN WAR TIME

10

Memory says: Want to do right? Don't count on me.
I'm a canal in Europe where bodies are floating
I'm a mass grave   I'm the life that returns
I'm a table set with room for the Stranger
I'm a field with corners left for the landless
I'm accused of child-death   of drinking blood
I'm a man-child praising God he's a man
I'm a woman bargaining for a chicken
I'm a woman who sells for a boat ticket
I'm a family dispersed between night and fog
I'm an immigrant tailor who says *A coat
is not a piece of cloth only*   I sway
in the learnings of the master-mystics
I have dreamed of Zion   I've dreamed of world revolution
I have dreamed my children could live at last like others
I have walked the children of others through ranks of hatred

I'm a corpse dredged from a canal in Berlin
a river in Mississippi   I'm a woman standing
with other women dressed in black
on the streets of Haifa, Tel Aviv, Jerusalem
there is spit on my sleeve there are phonecalls in the night
I am a woman standing in line for gasmasks
I stand on a road in Ramallah   with naked face   listening
I am standing here in your poem   unsatisfied
lifting my smoky mirror

1989–1990

TATTERED KADDISH

Taurean reaper of the wild apple field
messenger from earthmire gleaning
transcripts of fog
in the nineteenth year and the eleventh month
speak your tattered Kaddish for all suicides:

Praise to life though it crumbled in like a tunnel
on ones we knew and loved

     Praise to life though its windows blew shut
     on the breathing-room of ones we knew and loved

Praise to life though ones we knew and loved
loved it badly, too well, and not enough

     Praise to life though it tightened like a knot
     on the hearts of ones we thought we knew loved us

Praise to life giving room and reason
to ones we knew and loved who felt unpraisable

Praise to them, how they loved it, when they could.

1989

DARKLIGHT

I

Early day.   Grey the air.
Grey the boards of the house, the bench,
red the dilated potflower's petals
blue the sky that will rend through
this fog.
                    Dark summer's outer reaches:
thrown husk of a moon
sharpening
in the last dark blue.
I think of your eye
                        (dark the light
that washes into a deeper dark).

An eye, coming in closer.
                        Under the lens
lashes and veins grow huge
and huge the tear that washes out the eye,
the tear that clears the eye.

II

When heat leaves the walls at last
and the breeze comes
or seems to come, off water
or off the half-finished moon
her silver roughened by a darkblue rag
this is the ancient hour
between light and dark, work and rest
earthly tracks and star-trails
the last willed act of the day
and the night's first dream

If you could have this hour
for the last hour of your life.

1988–1990

FINAL NOTATIONS

it will not be simple, it will not be long
it will take little time, it will take all your thought
it will take all your heart, it will take all your breath
it will be short, it will not be simple

it will touch through your ribs, it will take all your heart
it will not be long, it will occupy your thought
as a city is occupied, as a bed is occupied
it will take all your flesh, it will not be simple

You are coming into us who cannot withstand you
you are coming into us who never wanted to withstand you
you are taking parts of us into places never planned
you are going far away with pieces of our lives

it will be short, it will take all your breath
it will not be simple, it will become your will

1991

from

DARK FIELDS
OF THE
REPUBLIC

(1995)

He had come a long way to this blue lawn,
and his dream must have seemed so close that
he could hardly fail to grasp it. He did not
know that it was already behind him, some-
where back in that vast obscurity beyond the
city, where the dark fields of the republic
rolled on under the night.

—*The Great Gatsby*

WHAT KIND OF TIMES ARE THESE

There's a place between two stands of trees where the grass grows
        uphill
and the old revolutionary road breaks off into shadows
near a meeting-house abandoned by the persecuted
who disappeared into those shadows.

I've walked there picking mushrooms at the edge of dread, but
        don't be fooled,
this isn't a Russian poem, this is not somewhere else but here,
our country moving closer to its own truth and dread,
its own ways of making people disappear.

I won't tell you where the place is, the dark mesh of the woods
meeting the unmarked strip of light—
ghost-ridden crossroads, leafmold paradise:
I know already who wants to buy it, sell it, make it disappear.

And I won't tell you where it is, so why do I tell you
anything? Because you still listen, because in times like these
to have you listen at all, it's necessary
to talk about trees.

1991

IN THOSE YEARS

In those years, people will say, we lost track
of the meaning of *we*, of *you*
we found ourselves
reduced to *I*
and the whole thing became
silly, ironic, terrible:
we were trying to live a personal life and, yes, that was the only life
we could bear witness to

But the great dark birds of history screamed and plunged
into our personal weather
They were headed somewhere else but their beaks and pinions drove
along the shore, through the rags of fog
where we stood, saying *I*

1991

CALLE VISIÓN

1

Not what you thought: just a turn-off
leading downhill not up

narrow, doesn't waste itself
has a house at the far end

scrub oak and cactus in the yard
some cats   some snakes

in the house there is a room
in the room there is a bed

on the bed there is a blanket
that tells the coming of the railroad

under the blanket there are sheets
scrubbed transparent here and there

under the sheets there's a mattress
the old rough kind, with buttons and ticking

under the mattress is a frame
of rusting iron   still strong

the whole bed smells of soap and rust
the window smells of old tobacco-dust and rain

this is your room
in Calle Visión

if you took the turn-off
it was for you

2

Calle Visión   sand in your teeth
granules of cartilage in your wrists

Calle Visión   firestorm behind
shuttered eyelids   fire in your foot

Calle Visión   rocking the gates
of your locked bones

Calle Visión   dreamnet dropped
over your porous sleep

3

Lodged in the difficult hotel
all help withheld

a place not to live but to die in
not an inn but a hospital

a friend's love came to me
touched and took me away

in a car   love
of a curmudgeon, a short-fuse

and as he drove   eyes on the road
I felt his love

and that was simply the case   the way things were
unstated and apparent

and like the rest of it
clear as a dream

4

Calle Visión   your heart beats on unbroken
   how is this possible

Calle Visión   wounded knee
   wounded spine   wounded eye

Have you ever worked around metal?
Are there particles under your skin?

Calle Visión   but your heart is still whole
   how is this possible

since what can be   will be taken
   when not offered in trust and faith

by the collectors of collectibles
   the professors of what-has-been-suffered

     The world is falling down   hold my hand
     It's a lonely sound   hold my hand

Calle Visión   never forget
   the body's pain

never divide it

5

Ammonia
        carbon dioxide
                carbon monoxide
                        methane
                hydrogen sulfide
:   the gasses that rise from urine and feces

in the pig confinement units known as nurseries
can eat a metal doorknob off in half a year

pig-dander
        dust from dry manure
—lung-scar: breath-shortedness an early symptom

And the fire shall try
every man's work   :Calle Visión:
and every woman's

if you took the turn-off
this is your revelation   this the source

6

The repetitive motions of slaughtering
        —fire in wrists   in elbows—
the dead birds coming at you along the line
        —how you smell them in your sleep—
fire in your wrist   blood packed
        under your fingernails   heavy air
doors padlocked on the outside
        —you might steal a chicken—
fire in the chicken factory fire
        in the carpal tunnel   leaping the frying vats
yellow smoke from soybean oil
        and wasted parts and insulating wire
—some fleeing to the freezer some
        found "stuck in poses of escape"—

7

You can call on beauty still and it will leap
from all directions

you can write beauty into the cruel file
of things done   things left undone   but

once we were dissimilar
yet unseparate   that's beauty   that's what you catch

in the newborn's midnight gaze
the fog that melts the falling stars

the virus from the smashed lianas driven
searching now for us

8

In the room   in the house
in Calle Visión

all you want   is to lie down
alone on your back   let your hands

slide lightly over your hipbones
But she's there with her remnants her cross-sections

trying to distract you
with her childhood her recipes her

cargo of charred pages her
carved and freckled neck-stones

her crying-out-for-witness her
backward-forward timescapes

her suitcase in Berlin
and the one lost and found

in her island go-and-come
—is she terrified you will forget her?

9

In the black net
of her orange wing

the angry nightblown butterfly
hangs on a piece of lilac in the sun

carried overland like her
from a long way off

She has travelled hard and far
and her interrogation goes:

—*Hands dripping with wet earth*
head full of shocking dreams

O what have you buried all these years
what have you dug up?

•

This place is alive with the dead and with the living
I have never been alone here

I wear my triple eye as I walk along the road
past, present, future all are at my side

Storm-beaten, tough-winged passenger
there is nothing I have buried that can die

10

On the road there is a house
scrub oak and cactus in the yard

lilac carried overland
from a long way off

in the house there is a bed
on the bed there is a blanket

telling the coming of the railroad
under the mattress there's a frame

of rusting iron   still strong
the window smells of old tobacco-dust and rain

the window smells of old
tobacco-dust and rain

1992–1993

TAKE

At the head of this poem I have laid out
a boning knife a paring knife a wooden spoon a pair of tongs.
Oaken grain beneath them olive and rusty light
around them.
And you looming: This is not your scene
this is the first frame of a film
I have in mind to make: move on, get out.
And you here telling me: What will be done
with these four objects will be done
through my lens not your words.

The poet shrugs: I was only in the kitchen
looking at the chopping board.   (Not the whole story.)

And you telling me: Awful is the scope
of what I have in mind, awful the music I shall deploy, most
awful the witness of the camera moving
out from the chopping board to the grains of snow
whirling against the windowglass to the rotating
searchlights of the tower.   The humped snow-shrouded tanks
laboring toward the border.   This is not your bookish art.

But say the poet picks up the boning knife and thinks *my bones*
if she touching the paring knife thinks *carrot, onion, celery*
if staring at the wooden spoon I see the wood is split
as if from five winters of war
when neither celery, onion, carrot could be found
or picking up the tongs I whisper *What this was for*

And did you say *get on, get out* or just *look out?*
Were you speaking from exhaustion from disaster from your last
          assignment were you afraid.
for the vision in the kitchen, that it could not be saved
—no time to unload the heavy
cases to adjust
the sensitive equipment
to seize the olive rusty light to scan the hand that reaches
          hovering
over a boning knife a paring knife a wooden spoon a pair
          of tongs
to cull the snow before it blows away across the border's blacked-
          out sheds
and the moon swims in a bluish bubble dimmed
by the rotating searchlights of the tower?   Here
it is in my shorthand, do what you have in mind.

1994

LATE GHAZAL

Footsole to scalp alive facing the window's black mirror.
First rains of the winter   morning's smallest hour.

Go back to the ghazal then   what will you do there?
Life always pulsed harder than the lines.

Do you remember the strands that ran from eye to eye?
The tongue that reached everywhere, speaking all the parts?

Everything there was cast in an image of desire.
The imagination's cry is a sexual cry.

I took my body anyplace with me.
In the thickets of abstraction my skin ran with blood.

Life was always stronger . . . the critics couldn't get it.
Memory says the music always ran ahead of the words.

1994

FROM PIERCÉD DARKNESS

New York/December

Taking the least griefcrusted avenue the last worst bridge away
somewhere beyond her Lost & Found we stopped in our flight to
         check backward
in the rearview mirror into her piercéd darkness.   A mirror is
         either flat or deep
and ours was deep to the vanishing point: we saw showroom

                    mannequins draped and trundled
—black lace across blackening ice—
false pearls knotted by nervous fingers, backribs lacquered in
                    sauce.
Narrow waters rocking in spasms.   The torch hand-held and the
                    poem of entrance.
Topless towers turned red and green.
Dripping faucet icicled radiator.
Eyes turned inward.   Births arced into dumpsters.
Eyes blazing under knitted caps,
hands gripped on taxi-wheels, steering.
Fir bough propped in a cardboard doorway, bitter tinsel.
The House of the Jewish Book, the Chinese Dumpling House.
Swaddled limbs dreaming on stacked shelves of sleep   opening
                    like knives.

    •

Her piercéd darkness.   Dragqueen dressed to kill in beauty
drawing her bridgelit shawls
over her shoulders.   Her caves ghosted by foxes.   Her tracked
                    arms.
Who climbs the subway stairs at the end of night
lugging a throwaway banquet.   Her
Man Who Lived Underground and all his children.
Nightcrews uncapping her streets wildlamps strung up on high.

    •

Fairy lights charming stunted trees.
Hurt eyes awake to the glamor.
I've walked this zone
gripping my nightstick, worked these rooms
in silver silk charmeuse and laid my offerings
next to the sexless swathed form lying in the doorway.
I've preached for justice rubbing crumbs
from sticky fingers for the birds.

Picked up a pretty chain of baubles
in the drugstore, bitten them to see if they were real.
I've boiled a stocking and called it Christmas pudding.
Bought freeborn eggs to cook
with sugar, milk and pears.

•

Altogether the angels arrive for the chorus
in rapidly grabbed robes they snatch scores of hallelujahs
complicit with television cameras they bend down their eyes.
However they sing their voices will glisten
in the soundmix.   All of it good enough for us.
Altogether children will wake before the end of night
("not good dawn" my Jewish grandmother called it) will stand
                as we did
handheld in cold dark before the parents' door
singing for glimpsed gilt and green
packages, the drama, the power of the hour.

•

Black lace, blackening ice.   To give on one designated day—
a window bangs shut on an entire
forcefield of chances, connections.   A window flies open
on the churning of birds in flight going surely somewhere else.
A snowflake like no other flies past, we will not hear of it
                again, we will surely
                hear of it
                again.

1994–1995

303

from

MIDNIGHT
SALVAGE

(1999)

I don't know how to measure happiness. The issue is happiness, there is no other issue, or no other issue one has a right to think about for other people, to think about politically, but I don't know how to measure happiness.

—George Oppen, letter to June Oppen Degnan,
August 5, 1970

THE ART OF TRANSLATION

1

To have seen you exactly, once:
red hair over cold cheeks fresh from the freeway
your lingo, your daunting and dauntless
eyes. But then to lift toward home, mile upon mile
back where they'd barely heard your name
—neither as terrorist nor as genius would they detain you—

to wing it back to my country bearing
your war-flecked protocols—

that was a mission, surely: my art's pouch
crammed with your bristling juices
sweet dark drops of your spirit
that streaked the pouch, the shirt I wore
and the bench on which I leaned.

2

It's only a branch like any other
green with the flare of life in it
and if I hold this end, you the other
that means it's broken

broken between us, broken despite us
broken and therefore dying
broken by force, broken by lying
green, with the flare of life in it

3

But say we're crouching on the ground like children
over a mess of marbles, soda caps, foil, old foreign coins
—the first truly precious objects. Rusty hooks, glass.

Say I saw the earring first but you wanted it.
Then you wanted the words I'd found. I'd give you
the earring, crushed lapis if it were,

I would look long at the beach glass and the sharded self
of the lightbulb. Long I'd look into your hand
at the obsolete copper profile, the cat's-eye, the lapis.

Like a thief I would deny the words, deny they ever
existed, were spoken, or could be spoken,
like a thief I'd bury them and remember where.

4

The trade names follow trade
the translators stopped at passport control:
Occupation: no such designation—
Journalist, maybe spy?

That the books are for personal use
only—could I swear it?
That not a word of them
is contraband—how could I prove it?

1995

FOR AN ANNIVERSARY

The wing of the osprey lifted
over the nest on Tomales Bay
into fog and difficult gust
raking treetops from Inverness Ridge on over
The left wing shouldered into protective
gesture the left wing we thought broken

and the young beneath in the windy nest
creaking there in their hunger
and the tides beseeching, besieging
the bay in its ruined languor

1996

MIDNIGHT SALVAGE

1

Up skyward through a glazed rectangle I
sought the light of a so-called heavenly body
: : a planet or our moon in some event and caught

nothing nothing but a late wind
pushing around some Monterey pines
themselves in trouble and rust-limbed

Nine o'clock : : July : the light
undrained : : that blotted blue
that lets has let will let

thought's blood ebb between life- and death-time
darkred behind darkblue
bad news pulsing back and forth of "us" and "them"

And all I wanted was to find an old
friend an old figure an old trigonometry
still true to our story in orbits flaming or cold

2

Under the conditions of my hiring
I could profess or declare anything at all
since in that place nothing would change
So many fountains, such guitars at sunset

Did not want any more to sit under such a window's
deep embrasure, wisteria bulging on spring air
in that borrowed chair
with its collegiate shield at a borrowed desk

under photographs of the spanish steps, Keats' death mask
and the English cemetery all so under control and so eternal
in burnished frames : : or occupy the office
of the marxist-on-sabbatical

with Gramsci's fast-fading eyes
thumbtacked on one wall opposite a fading print
of the same cemetery : : had memories
and death masks of my own : : could not any more

peruse young faces already straining for
the production of slender testaments
to swift reading and current thinking : : would not wait
for the stroke of noon to declare all passions obsolete

Could not play by the rules
in that palmy place : : nor stand at lectern professing
anything at all
                    in their hire

3

Had never expected hope would form itself
completely in my time : : was never so sanguine
as to believe old injuries could transmute easily
through any singular event or idea : : never
so feckless as to ignore the managed contagion
of ignorance the contrived discontinuities
the felling of leaders and future leaders
the pathetic erections of soothsayers

But thought I was conspiring, breathing-along
with history's systole-diastole
twenty thousand leagues under the sea a mammal heartbeat
sheltering another heartbeat
plunging from the Farallons all the way to Baja
sending up here or there a blowhole signal
and sometimes beached
making for warmer waters
where the new would be delivered : : though I would not see it

4

But neither was expecting in my time
to witness this : : wasn't deep
lucid or mindful you might say enough
to look through history's bloodshot eyes
into this commerce this dreadnought wreck cut loose

from all vows, oaths, patents, compacts, promises : :

>   To see

not O my Captain
fallen cold & dead by the assassin's hand

but cold alive & cringing : : drinking with the assassins
in suit of noir Hong Kong silk
pushing his daughter in her famine-
waisted flamingo gown
out on the dance floor with the traffickers
in nerve gas saying to them *Go for it*
and to the girl *Get with it*

5

When I ate and drank liberation once I walked
arm-in-arm with someone who said she had something to teach me
It was the avenue and the dwellers
free of home : roofless : : women
without pots to scour or beds to make
or combs to run through hair
or hot water for lifting grease or cans
to open or soap to slip in that way
under arms then beneath breasts then downward to thighs

Oil-drums were alight under the freeway
and bottles reached from pallets of cardboard corrugate
and piles of lost and found to be traded back and forth
and figures arranging themselves from the wind
Through all this she walked me : : And said
My name is Liberation and I come from here
Of what are you afraid?

We've hung late in the bars like bats
kissed goodnight at the stoplights
—did you think I wore this city without pain?
did you think I had no family?

6

Past the curve where the old craftsman was run down
there's a yard called Midnight Salvage
He was walking in the road which was always safe
The young driver did not know that road
its curves or that people walked there
or that you could speed yet hold the curve
watching for those who walked there
such skills he did not have being in life unpracticed

but I have driven that road in madness and driving rain
thirty years in love and pleasure and grief-blind
on ice I have driven it and in the vague haze of summer
between clumps of daisies and sting of fresh cowflop odors
lucky I am I hit nobody old or young
killed nobody left no trace
practiced in life as I am

7

This horrible patience which is part of the work
This patience which waits for language for meaning for the
            least sign
This encumbered plodding state doggedly dragging
the IV up and down the corridor
with the plastic sack of bloodstained urine

Only so can you start living again
waking to take the temperature of the soul
when the black irises lean at dawn
from the mouth of the bedside pitcher
This condition in which you swear *I will
submit to whatever poetry is
I accept no limits*   Horrible patience

8

You cannot eat an egg   You don't know where it's been
The ordinary body of the hen
vouchsafes no safety   The countryside refuses to supply
Milk is powdered   meat's in both senses high

Old walls the pride of architects   collapsing
find us in crazed niches   sleeping like foxes
we wanters we unwanted we
wanted for the crime of being ourselves

Fame slides on its belly like any other animal after food
Ruins are disruptions of system leaking in
weeds and light   redrawing
the City of Expectations

You cannot eat an egg   Unstupefied not unhappy
we braise wild greens and garlic   feed the feral cats
and when the fog's irregular documents break open
scan its fissures for young stars
                   in the belt of Orion

1996

SHATTERED HEAD

A life hauls itself uphill
    through hoar-mist steaming
the sun's tongue licking
    leaf upon leaf into stricken liquid
When?   *When?* cry the soothseekers
    but time is a bloodshot eye
seeing its last of beauty its own
    foreclosure
                        a bloodshot mind
finding itself unspeakable
    What is the last thought?
Now I will let you know?
    or, *Now I know?*
(porridge of skull-splinters, brain tissue
    mouth and throat membrane, cranial fluid)

Shattered head on the breast
    of a wooded hill
laid down there endlessly so
    tendrils soaked into matted compost
become a root
    torqued over the faint springhead
groin whence illegible
    matter leaches: worm-borings, spurts of silt
volumes of sporic changes
    hair long blown into far follicles
blasted into a chosen place

Revenge on the head (genitals, breast, untouched)
    revenge on the mouth
packed with its inarticulate confessions

revenge on the eyes
green-gray and restless
      revenge on the big and searching lips
                  the tender tongue
revenge on the sensual, on the nose the
     carrier of history
revenge on the life devoured
in another incineration

You can walk by such a place, the earth is made of them
where the stretched tissue of a field or woods is humid
          with belovéd matter
the soothseekers have withdrawn
you feel no ghost, only a sporic chorus
when that place utters its worn sigh
    let us have peace

And the shattered head answers back
    I believed I was loved, I believed I loved,
      who did this to us?

1996–97

CAMINO REAL

Hot stink of skunk
crushed at the vineyards' edge

hawk-skied, carrion-clean
clouds ranging themselves
over enormous autumn

that scribble   edged and skunky
as the great road winds on
toward my son's house seven hours south

Walls of the underpass
smudged and blistered eyes gazing from armpits
THE WANTER WANTED   ARMED IN LOVE AND
          DANGEROUS
WANTED FOR WANTING

To become the scholar of : :
: : to list compare contrast events to footnote lesser evils
calmly to note "bedsprings"
describe how they were wired
to which parts of the body
to make clear-eyed assessments of the burnt-out eye: :
investigate
the mouth-bit and the mouth
the half-swole slippery flesh the enforced throat
the whip they played you with the backroad games the beatings by
          the river
O to list collate commensurate to quantify:
I was the one, I suffered, I was there

never
to trust to memory only

to go back   notebook in hand
dressed as no one there was dressed

over and over to quantify
on a gridded notebook page

The difficulty of proving
such things were done for no reason
that every night
"in those years"
people invented reasons for torture

Asleep now,   head in hands
hands over ears   O you
Who do this work
every one of you
every night

Driving south: santabarbara's barbarous
landscaped mind: lest it be forgotten
in the long sweep downcoast

let it not be exonerated

but O the light
on the raw Pacific silks

Charles Olson: "Can you afford not to make
                        the magical study
                            which happiness is?"

I take him to mean
that happiness is in itself a magical study
a glimpse of the *unhandicapped life*
as it might be for anyone, somewhere

a kind of alchemy, a study of transformation
else it withers, wilts

—that happiness is not to be
mistrusted or wasted
though it ferment in grief

George Oppen to June Degnan: "I don't know how
to measure happiness"
—Why measure? in itself it's the measure—
at the end of a day
        of great happiness if there be such a day

drawn by love's unprovable pull

I write this, sign it
                        Adrienne

1997

SEVEN SKINS

1

Walk along back of the library
in 1952
someone's there to catch your eye
Vic Greenberg in his wheelchair
paraplegic GI—
Bill of Rights Jew
graduate student going in
by the only elevator route
up into the great stacks where
all knowledge should and is

and shall be stored like sacred grain
while the loneliest of lonely
American decades goes aground
on the postwar rock
and some unlikely
shipmates found ourselves
stuck amid so many smiles

Dating Vic Greenberg you date
crutches and a chair
a cool wit an outrageous form:
"—just back from a paraplegics' conference,
guess what the biggest meeting was about—
Sex with a Paraplegic!—for the wives—"
In and out of cabs his chair
opening and closing round his
electrical monologue the air
furiously calm around him
as he transfers to the crutches

But first you go for cocktails
in his room at Harvard
he mixes the usual martinis, plays Billie Holiday
talks about Melville's vision of evil
and the question of the postwar moment:
Is there an American civilization?
In the bathroom huge
grips and suction-cupped
rubber mats long-handled sponges
the reaching tools a veteran's benefits
in plainest sight

And this is only memory, no more
so this is how you remember

Vic Greenberg takes you to the best restaurant
which happens to have no stairs
for talk about movies, professors, food
Vic orders wine and tastes it
you have lobster, he Beef Wellington
the famous dessert is baked alaska
ice cream singed in a flowerpot
from the oven, a live tulip inserted there

Chair to crutches, crutches to cab
chair in the cab and back to Cambridge
memory shooting its handheld frames
Shall I drop you, he says, or shall
we go back to the room for a drink?
It's the usual question
a man has to ask it
a woman has to answer
you don't even think

2

What a girl I was then what a body
ready for breaking open like a lobster
what a little provincial village
what a hermit crab seeking nobler shells
what a beach of rattling stones what an offshore raincloud
what a gone-and-come tidepool

what a look into eternity I took and did not return it
what a book I made myself
what a quicksilver study
bright little bloodstain
liquid pouches escaping

What a girl pelican-skimming over fear what a mica lump
        splitting
into tiny sharp-edged mirrors through which
the sun's eclipse could seem normal
what a sac of eggs what a drifting flask
eager to sink   to be found
to disembody   what a mass of swimmy legs

3

Vic into what shoulder could I have pushed your face
laying hands first on your head
onto whose thighs pulled down your head
which fear of mine would have wound itself
around which of yours   could we have taken it   nakedness
without sperm   in what insurrectionary
convulsion would we have done it   mouth to mouth
mouth-tongue to vulva-tongue to anus   earlobe to nipple
what seven skins each have to molt what seven shifts
what tears boil up through sweat to bathe
what humiliatoriums   what layers of imposture

What heroic tremor
released into pure moisture
might have soaked our shape   two-headed   avid
into your heretic
linen-service
sheets?

1997

from

FOX

(2001)

REGARDLESS

An idea declared itself between us
clear as a washed wineglass
that we'd love
regardless of manifestos I wrote or signed
my optimism of the will
regardless
your wincing at manifestos
your practice of despair you named
anarchism
: : an idea we could meet
somewhere else   a road
straggling unmarked through ice-plant
toward an ocean   heartless as eternity

Still hungry for freedom   I walked off
from glazed documents   becalmed
passions   time of splintering and sawdust
pieces lying still   I was not myself but
I found a road like that   it straggled
The ocean still
looked like eternity
I drew it on a
napkin mailed it to you

On your hands you wear work gloves stiffened
in liquids your own body has expressed
: : what stiffens hardest?   tears? blood? urine? sweat? the first
     drops from the penis?
Your glove then meets my hand   this is our meeting
Which of us has gone furthest?

To meet you like this I've had to rise
from love in a room
of green leaves larger than my clitoris or my brain

in a climate where winter never precisely
does or does not engrave its name on the windowpane
while the Pacific lays down its right of way
to the other side of the world

: : to a table where singed manifestos
curl back crying to be reread

but can I even provoke you
joking or
in tears
you   in long-stiffened gloves   still
protector of despair?

For H.C.

1998–1999

FOX

I needed fox   Badly I needed
a vixen for the long time none had come near me
I needed recognition from a
triangulated face   burnt-yellow eyes
fronting the long body the fierce and sacrificial tail
I needed history of fox   briars of legend it was said she had run through
I was in want of fox

And the truth of briars she had to have run through
I craved to feel on her pelt   if my hands could even slide
past or her body slide between them   sharp truth distressing surfaces
    of fur

lacerated skin calling legend to account
a vixen's courage in vixen terms

For a human animal to call for help
on another animal
is the most riven the most revolted cry on earth
come a long way down
Go back far enough it means tearing and torn   endless and sudden
back far enough it blurts
into the birth-yell of the yet-to-be human child
pushed out of a female   the yet-to-be woman

1998

NOCTILUCENT CLOUDS

Late night on the underside   a spectral glare
abnormal   Everything below
must and will betray itself
as a floodlit truckstop out here
on the North American continent stands revealed
and we're glad because it's late evening and no town
but this, diesel, regular, soda, coffee, chips, beer and video
no government no laws but LIGHT in the continental dark
and then   and then   what smallness the soul endures
rolling out on the ramp from such an isle
onto the harborless Usonian plateau

Dear Stranger   can I raise a poem
to justice   you not here
with your sheet-lightning apprehension
of nocturne

your surveyor's eye for distance
as if any forest's fallen tree were for you
a possible hypotenuse

Can I wake as I once woke with no thought of you
into the bad light of a futureless motel

This thing I am calling justice:
I could slide my hands into your leather gloves
but my feet would not fit into your boots

Every art leans on some other: yours
on mine in spasm retching
last shreds of vanity
We swayed together like cripples when the wind
suddenly turned a corner   or was it we who turned

Once more I invite you into this
in retrospect it will be clear

1999

IF YOUR NAME IS ON THE LIST

If your name is on the list of judges
you're one of them
though you fought their hardening
assumptions   went and stood
alone by the window while they
concurred
It wasn't enough to hold your singular
minority opinion

You had to face the three bridges
down the river
your old ambitions
flamboyant in bloodstained mist

You had to carry off under arm
and write up in perfect loneliness
your soul-splitting dissent

Yes, I know a soul can be partitioned like a country
In all the new inhere old judgments
loyalties crumbling send up sparks and smoke
We want to be part of the future   dragging in
what pure futurity can't use

Suddenly a narrow street a little beach a little century
screams   *Don't let me go*

Don't let me die   Do you forget
what we were to each other

1999

TERZA RIMA

1

Hail-spurting sky   sun
splashing off persimmons left
in the quit garden

of the quit house   The realtor's swaying name
against this cloudheap this
surrendered acre

I would   so help me   tell you if I could
how some great teacher
came to my side and said:

Let's go down   into the underworld
—the earth already crazed
Let me take your hand

—but who would that be?
already trembling on the broken crust
who would I trust?

I become the default derailed memory-raided
limping
teacher I never had   I lead and   I follow

2

Call it the earthquake trail:
I lead through live-oak meadows
to the hillside   where the plates shuddered

rewind the seismic story
point to the sundered
fence of 1906   the unmatching rocks

trace the loop under dark bay branches
blurred with moss
behaving like a guide

Like a novice I lag
behind with the little snake
dead on the beaten path

This will never happen again

3

At the end of the beaten path we're sold free
tickets for the celebration
of the death of history

The last page of the calendar
will go up   a sheet of flame
(no one will be permitted on the bridge)

We'll assemble by letters
alphabetical
each ticket a letter

to view ourselves as giants
on screen-surround
in the parking lot

figures of men and women firmly pushing
babies in thickly padded prams
through disintegrating malls

into the new era

4

I have lost our way   the fault is mine
ours   the fault belongs
to us   I become   the guide

who should have defaulted
who should have remained the novice
I   as guide   failed

I as novice   trembled
I should have been stronger   held us
together

5

I thought I was
stronger   my will the ice-sail
speeding my runners

along frozen rivers
bloodied by sunset
thought I could be forever

will-ful   my sail filled
with perfect ozone   my blades
flashing clean into the ice

6

Was that youth?   that clear
sapphire on snow
a distinct hour

in Central Park   that smell
on sidewalk and windowsill
fresh and unmixt

the blizzard's peace and drama
over the city
a public privacy

                    waiting
in the small steamed-up copy shop
slush tracked in across a wooden floor

then shivering   elated
in twilight
at the bus stop   with others   a public happiness

7

Not simple is it to do
a guide's work   the novices
irrupting hourly with their own bad vigor

knowing not who they are
every phase of moon an excuse
for fibrillating

besides the need   in today's world
to consider
outreach   the new thinking

—Or: love will strongly move you
or commerce will
You want a priest?   go to the altar

where eternal bargains are struck
want love?
go down inside your destructible heart

8

In Almodóvar's film
we go for truth to the prostitutes' field
to find past and future

elegant   beaten-up and knifed
sex without gender
preyed-on and preying

transactions   zones of play
the circling drivers
in search of their desires

theater of love   Ninth Circle
there are so many teachers
here   no fire can shrink them

*Do you understand?   you could get your face
slashed in such a place
Do you think this is a movie?*

9

She says: I gave my name and it was taken
I no longer have my name
I gave my word and it was broken

My words are learning
to walk on crutches
through traffic

without stammering
My name is a prisoner
who will not name names

She says: I gave my tongue
to love   and this
makes it hard to speak

She says: When my life depended
on one of two
opposite terms

I dared mix beauty with courage
they were my lovers
together they were tortured

10

Sick of my own old poems   caught
on rainshower Fifth Avenue
in a bookstore

I reach to a shelf
and there you are   Pier Paolo
speaking to Gramsci's ashes

in the old encircling rhyme
Vivo nel non volere
del tramontato dopoguerra:

                    amando
il mondo che odio . . .
that vernacular voice
intimately political

and that was how you died
so I clasp my book to my heart
as the shop closes

11

Under the blackened dull-metal corners
of the small espresso pot
a jet flares blue

a smell tinctures the room
—some sniff or prescience of
a life that actually could be

lived   a grain of hope
a bite of bitter chocolate in the subway
to pull on our senses

without them we're prey
to the failed will
its science of despair

12

How I hate it when you ascribe to me
a "woman's vision"
cozy with coffeepots   drawn curtains

or   leaning in black leather dress
over your chair
black fingernail tracing your lines

overspent Sibyl drifting in a bottle

How I've hated speaking "as a woman"
for mere continuation
when the broken is what I saw

As a woman   do I love
and hate?   as a woman
do I munch my bitter chocolate underground?

Yes.   No.   You too
sexed as you are   hating
this whole thing   you keep on   it remaking

13

Where the novice pulls the guide
across frozen air
where the guide suddenly grips   the shoulder

of the novice   where the moss is golden
the sky sponged with pink at sunset
where the urine of reindeer barely vanished

stings the air like a sharp herb
where the throat of the clear-cut opens
across the surrendered forest

I'm most difficultly
with you   I lead
and I follow

our shadows   reindeer-huge
slip onto the map
of chance and purpose   figures

on the broken crust
exchanging places   bites to eat
a glance

2000

RAUSCHENBERG'S BED

How a bed once dressed with a kindly quilt becomes
unsleepable site of anarchy   What body holes expressed
their exaltation loathing exhaustion
what horse of night has pawed those sheets
what talk under the blanket raveled
what clitoris lain very still in her own subversion
what traveler homeward reached for familiar bedding
and felt stiff tatters under his fingers
How a bed is horizontal yet this is vertical
inarticulate liquids spent from a spectral pillow

How on a summer night someone drives out on the roads
while another one lies ice-packed in dreams of freezing

Sometimes this bed has eyes, sometimes breasts
sometimes eking forth from its laden springs
pity compassion pity again for all they have worn and borne
Sometimes it howls for penis sometimes vagina sometimes
for the nether hole the everywhere

How the children sleep and wake
the children   sleep awake upstairs

How on a single night the driver of roads comes back
into the sweat-cold bed of the dreamer

leans toward what's there for warmth
human limbs   human crust

2000

WAITING FOR YOU AT THE MYSTERY SPOT

I sat down facing the steep place where
tours clambered upward and others straggled down, the redwoods
    outstanding all
A family, East Asian, holding a picnic at their van:
"We are always hungry," the older sister said laughing, "and we
    always bring our food"
Roses clambered a rough fence in the slanting sun that speared
    the redwoods
We'd gone into the gift shop while waiting for your tour
found Davy Crockett coonskin caps, deerskin coin purses
scorpions embedded in plastic, MYSTERY SPOT bumper stickers
and postcards of men you wouldn't be left alone with
a moment if you could help it, illustrating
the Mystery Spot and its tricks with gravity and horizon
Your tour was called and you started upward.   I went back
to my redwood bench
                  "The *mystai* streamed"
                              toward the

      mystery

But if anything up there was occult
nothing at ground level was: tiny beings flashing around
in the sun secure knowing their people were nearby
grandfathers, aunts, elder brothers or sisters, parents and loved friends
You could see how it was when each tour was called and gathered itself
who rode on what shoulders, ran alongside, held hands
the languages all different, English the least of these
I sat listening to voices watching the miraculous migration
of sunshafts through the redwoods   the great spears folding up
into letters from the sun deposited through dark green slots
each one saying
                    I love you but
I must draw away   Believe, I will return

Then: happiness! your particular figures
in the descending crowd: Anne, Jacob, Charlie!
Anne with her sandals off
in late day warmth and odor and odd wonder

2000

from

THE SCHOOL
AMONG
THE RUINS

(2004)

CENTAUR'S REQUIEM

Your hooves drawn together underbelly
shoulders in mud   your mane
of wisp and soil deporting all the horse of you

your longhaired neck
eyes   jaw yes   and ears
unforgivably human on such a creature
unforgivably what you are
deposited in the grit-kicked field of a champion

tender neck and nostrils   teacher   water-lily suction-spot
what you were   marvelous   we could not stand

Night drops   an awaited storm
driving in to wreck your path
Foam on your hide like flowers
where you fell   or fall   desire

2001

EQUINOX

Time split like a fruit between dark and light
and a usual fog drags
over this landfall
I've walked September end to end
barefoot room to room
carrying in hand a knife well honed for cutting stem or root
                        or wick   eyes open
to abalone shells   memorial candle flames

split lemons   roses laid
                      along charring logs   Gorgeous things
: : dull acres of developed land as we had named it: Nowhere
wetland   burnt garbage looming at its heart
gunmetal thicket   midnightblue blood and
                      tricking masks   I thought I knew
history was not a novel

So can I say it was not I   listed as Innocence
betrayed you   serving (and protesting always)
the motives of my government
thinking we'd scratch out a place
where poetry   old subversive shape
grew out of Nowhere   here?
where skin could lie on skin
a place "outside the limits"

                Can say I was mistaken?

To be so bruised: in the soft organs   skeins of consciousness
Over and over have let it be
damage to others   crushing of the animate core
that tone-deaf cutloose ego swarming the world

so bruised: heart   spleen   long inflamed ribbons of the guts
the spine's vertical necklace swaying

Have let it swarm
through us   let it happen
as it must, inmost

but before this: long before this   those other eyes
frontally exposed themselves and spoke

2001

TELL ME

1

Tell me, why way toward dawn the body
close to a body familiar as itself
chills—tell me, is this the hour
                    remembered if outlived
as freezing—no, don't tell me

Dreams spiral birdwinged overhead
a peculiar hour   the silver mirror-frame's
quick laugh the caught light-lattice on the wall
as a truck drives off before dawn
headlights on

Not wanting
to *write this up*   for the public   not wanting
to *write it down*   in secret

just to lie here in this cold story
feeling it   trying to feel it through

2

Blink and smoke, flicking with absent nail
                              at the mica bar
where she refills without asking
Crouch into your raingarb   this will be a night
unauthorized shock troops are abroad

this will be a night
the face-ghosts lean
                    over the banister

declaring the old stories all
froze like beards or frozen margaritas
all the new stories taste of lukewarm
margaritas, lukewarm kisses

3

From whence I draw this: *harrowed in defeats of language*
in history to my barest marrow
This: one syllable then another
gropes upward
one stroke laid on another
sound from one throat then another
never in the making
making beauty or sense

always mis-taken, draft, roughed-in
only to be struck out
is blurt is roughed-up
hot keeps body
in leaden hour
simmering

2001

THE SCHOOL AMONG THE RUINS

Beirut.Baghdad.Sarajevo.Bethlehem.Kabul. Not of course here.

1

Teaching the first lesson and the last
—great falling light of summer will you last
longer than schooltime?
When children flow
in columns at the doors
BOYS GIRLS and the busy teachers

open or close high windows
with hooked poles   drawing darkgreen shades

closets unlocked, locked
questions unasked, asked, when

love of the fresh impeccable
sharp-pencilled   yes
order without cruelty

a street on earth   neither heaven nor hell
busy with commerce and worship
young teachers walking to school

fresh bread and early-open foodstalls

2

When the offensive rocks the sky when nightglare
misconstrues day and night when lived-in
rooms from the upper city
tumble cratering lower streets

cornices of olden ornament   human debris
when fear vacuums out the streets

When the whole town flinches
blood on the undersole thickening to glass

Whoever crosses   hunched   knees bent   a contested zone
knows why she does this suicidal thing

School's now in session day and night
children sleep
in the classrooms   teachers rolled close

3

How the good teacher loved
his school   the students
the lunchroom with fresh sandwiches

lemonade and milk
the classroom   glass cages
of moss and turtles
teaching responsibility

A morning breaks without bread or fresh-poured milk
parents or lesson plans

diarrhea first question of the day
children shivering   it's September
Second question: where is my mother?

4

One: I don't know where your mother
is   Two: I don't know
why they are trying to hurt us
Three: or the latitude and longitude
of their hatred   Four: I don't know if we
hate them as much   I think there's more toilet paper
in the supply closet   I'm going to break it open

Today this is your lesson:
write as clearly as you can
your name   home street   and number
down on this page
No you can't go home yet
but you aren't lost
this is our school

I'm not sure what we'll eat
we'll look for healthy roots and greens
searching for water though the pipes are broken

5

There's a young cat sticking
her head through window bars
she's hungry like us
but can feed on mice
her bronze erupting fur
speaks of a life already wild

her golden eyes
don't give quarter   She'll teach us   Let's call her
Sister
when we get milk we'll give her some

6

I've told you, let's try to sleep in this funny camp
All night pitiless pilotless things go shrieking
above us to somewhere

Don't let your faces turn to stone
Don't stop asking me why
Let's pay attention to our cat   she needs us

Maybe tomorrow the bakers can fix their ovens

7

"We sang them to naps   told stories   made
shadow-animals with our hands

wiped human debris off boots and coats
sat learning by heart the names
some were too young to write
some had forgotten how"

2001

THIS EVENING LET'S

not talk

about my country   How
I'm from an optimistic culture

that speaks louder than my passport
Don't double-agent-contra my

invincible innocence   I've
got my own

suspicions   Let's
order retsina

cracked olives and bread
I've got questions of my own but

let's give a little
let's let a little be

If *friendship is not a tragedy*
if it's a mercy

we can be merciful
if it's just escape

we're neither of us running
why otherwise be here

Too many reasons not
to waste a rainy evening

in a backroom of bouzouki
and kitchen Greek

I've got questions of my own but
let's let it be a little

There's a beat in my head
song of my country

called Happiness, U.S.A.
Drowns out bouzouki

drowns out world and fusion
with its *Get—get—get*

into your happiness before
happiness pulls away

hangs a left along the piney shore
weaves a hand at you—"one I adore"—

Don't be proud, run hard for that
enchantment boat

tear up the shore if you must but
get into your happiness because

before
and otherwise
it's going to pull away

So tell me later
what I know already

and what I don't get
yet   save for another day

Tell me this time
what you are going through

travelling the Metropolitan
Express

break out of that style
give me your smile
awhile

2001

THE EYE

A balcony, violet shade on stucco   fruit in a plastic bowl on the iron
     raggedy legged table, grapes and sliced melon, saucers, a knife, wine
in a couple of thick short tumblers cream cheese once came in: our snack
     in the eye of the war   There are places where fruit is implausible, even
rest is implausible, places where wine if any should be poured into wounds
     but we're not yet there or it's not here yet   it's the war
not us, that moves, pauses and hurtles forward into the neck
     and groin of the city, the soft indefensible places but not here yet

Behind the balcony an apartment, papers, pillows, green vines still watered
     there are waterless places but not here yet, there's a bureau topped
                                        with marble
and combs and brushes on it, little tubes for lips and eyebrows, a dish
                                        of coins and keys

there's a bed a desk a stove a cane rocker a bookcase civilization
cage with a skittery bird, there are birdless places but not
    here yet, this bird must creak and flutter in the name of all
uprooted orchards, limbless groves
    this bird standing for wings and song that here can't fly

Our bed quilted   wine poured   future uncertain   you'd think
    people like us would have it scanned and planned   tickets to somewhere
would be in the drawer   with all our education you'd think we'd
                                    have taken measures
    soon as ash started turning up on the edges of everything ash
in the leaves of books ash on the leaves of trees and in the veins of
                                    the passive
    innocent life we were leading calling it hope
you'd think that and we thought this   it's the war not us that's moving
    like shade on a balcony

2002

THERE IS NO ONE STORY AND ONE STORY ONLY

The engineer's story of hauling coal
to Davenport for the cement factory, sitting on the bluffs
between runs looking for whales, hauling concrete
back to Gilroy, he and his wife renewing vows
in the glass chapel in Arkansas after 25 years
The flight attendant's story murmured
to the flight steward in the dark galley
of her fifth-month loss of nerve
about carrying the baby she'd seen on the screen
The story of the forensic medical team's
small plane landing on an Alaska icefield
of the body in the bag they had to drag

over the ice like the whole life of that body
The story of the man driving
600 miles to be with a friend in another country   seeming
easy when leaving but afterward
writing in a letter difficult truths
Of the friend watching him leave remembering
the story of her body
with his once and the stories of their children
made with other people and how his mind went on
pressing hers like a body
There is the story of the mind's
temperature neither cold nor celibate
Ardent   The story of
not one thing only.

2002

TRANSPARENCIES

That the meek word like the righteous word can bully
that an Israeli soldier interviewed years
after the first Intifada could mourn on camera
what under orders he did, saw done, did not refuse
that another leaving Beit Jala could scrawl
on a wall: *We are truely sorry for the mess we made*
is merely routine   word that would cancel deed
That human equals innocent and guilty
That we grasp for innocence whether or no
is elementary   That words can translate into broken bones
That the power to hurl words is a weapon
That the body can be a weapon
any child on playground knows   That asked your favorite word
                                                            in a game

you always named a thing, a quality, *freedom* or *river*
(never a pronoun never *God* or *War*)
is taken for granted   That word and body
are all we have to lay on the line
That words are windowpanes in a ransacked hut, smeared
by time's dirty rains, we might argue
likewise that words are clear as glass till the sun strikes it blinding

But that in a dark windowpane you have seen your face
That when you wipe your glasses the text grows clearer
That the sound of crunching glass comes at the height of the
                                        wedding
That I can look through glass
into my neighbor's house
but not my neighbor's life
That glass is sometimes broken to save lives

That a word can be crushed like a goblet underfoot
is only what it seems, part question, part answer: how
                              you live it

2002

MEMORIZE THIS

i

Love for twenty-six years, you can't stop
A withered petunia's crisp   the bud sticky   both are dark
The flower engulfed in its own purple   So common, nothing
                                        like it

The old woodstove gone to the dump
Sun plunges through the new skylight
This morning's clouds piled like autumn in Massachusetts
This afternoon's far-flung like the Mojave
Night melts one body into another
One drives fast the other maps a route
Thought new it becomes familiar
From thirteen years back maybe
One oils the hinges one edges the knives
One loses an earring the other finds it
One says I'd rather make love
Than go to the Greek Festival
The other, I agree.

ii

Take a strand of your hair
on my fingers let it fall
across the pillow   lift to my nostrils
inhale your body entire

Sleeping with you after
weeks apart   how normal
yet   after midnight
to turn and slide my arm
along your thigh
drawn up in sleep
what delicate amaze

2002–2003

SCREEN DOOR

Metallic slam on a moonless night
A short visit and so we departed.
A short year with many long
                                        days
A long phone call with many   pauses.
                        It was gesture's code
we were used to using, we were
                                        awkward without it.

Over the phone: knocking heard
at a door in another country.
Here it's tonight: there tomorrow.
A vast world we used to think small.
That we knew everyone who mattered.

Firefly flicker.   Metallic slam.   A moonless night.   Too dark
                                        for gesture.
But it was gesture's code we were used to.
                                        Might need again.   Urgent
                                        hold-off or beckon.

Fierce supplication. One finger pointing: "Thither."
Palms flung upward: "What now?"
Hand slicing the air or across the throat.
A long wave to the departing.

2003

from

TELEPHONE RINGING IN THE LABYRINTH

(2007)

Poetry isn't easy to come by.
You have to write it like you owe a debt to the world.
In that way poetry is how the world comes to be in you.

—Alan Davies

Poetry is not self-expression, the I is a dramatic I.

—Michael S. Harper, quoting Sterling A. Brown

To which I would add: and so, unless
otherwise indicated, is the You.

—A.R.

CALIBRATIONS

She tunes her guitar for Landstuhl
where she will sit on beds and sing
ballads from when Romany
roamed Spain

•

A prosthetic hand calibrates perfectly
the stem of a glass
or how to stroke a face
is this how far we have come
to make love easy

Ghost limbs go into spasm in the night
You come back from war with the body you have

•

What you can't bear
carry endure lift
you'll have to drag

it'll come with you the ghostlimb

the shadow   blind
echo of your body spectre of your soul

•

Let's not talk yet of making love
nor of ingenious devices
replacing touch

And this is not theoretical:
A poem with calipers to hold a heart
so it will want to go on beating

2004

SKELETON KEY

In the marina an allegro creaking
boats on the tide
each with its own sway
                      rise and fall
acceptance and refusal
La Barqueta, My Pelican

barometer in the body
rising and falling

•

A small wound, swallow-shaped, on my wrist
ripped by a thorn
exacerbated by ash and salt

And this is how I came to be
protector of the private
and enemy of the personal

•

Then I slept, and had a dream
No more
No màs

From now on, only
reason's drugged and dreamless sleep

•

Creeps down the rockface   shadow cast
from an opposite crag exactly at that moment
you needed light on the trail   These are the shortening days
you forgot about   bent on your own design

•

Cut me a skeleton key
to that other time, that city
talk starting up, deals and poetry

Tense with elation, exiles
walking old neighborhoods
calm journeys of streetcars

revived boldness of cats
locked eyes of couples
music playing full blast again

Exhuming the dead   Their questions

2004

BEHIND THE MOTEL

A man lies under a car half bare
a child plays bullfight with a torn cloth
hemlocks grieve in wraps of mist
a woman talks on the phone, looks in a mirror
fiddling with the metal pull of a drawer

She has seen her world wiped clean, the cloth
that wiped it disintegrate in mist
or dying breath on the skin of a mirror
She has felt her life close like a drawer
has awoken somewhere else, bare

He feels his skin as if it were mist
as if his face would show in no mirror
He needs some bolts he left in a vanished drawer
crawls out into the hemlocked world with his bare
hands, wipes his wrench on an oil-soaked cloth

stares at the woman talking into a mirror
who has shut the phone into the drawer
while over and over with a torn cloth
at the edge of hemlocks behind the bare
motel a child taunts a horned beast made from mist

2004

ARCHAIC

Cold wit leaves me cold
this time of the world   Multifoliate disorders
straiten my gait   Minuets don't become me
Been wanting to get out   see the sights
but the exits are slick with people
going somewhere fast
every one with a shared past
and a mot juste   And me so out of step
with my late-night staircase inspirations   my
utopian slant

Still, I'm alive here
in this village drawn in a tightening noose
of ramps and cloverleafs
but the old directions I drew up
for you
are obsolete

Here's how
to get to me
I wrote
Don't misconstrue the distance
take along something for the road
everything might be closed
this isn't a modern place

You arrived starving at midnight
I gave you warmed-up food
poured tumblers of brandy
put on Les Barricades Mystérieuses
—the only jazz in the house
We talked for hours   of barricades
lesser and greater sorrows
ended up laughing in the thicksilver
birdstruck light

2005

LONG AFTER STEVENS

A locomotive pushing through snow in the mountains
more modern than the will

to be modern   The mountain's profile
in undefiled snow disdains

definitions of poetry   It was always
indefinite, task and destruction

the laser eye of the poet   her blind eye
her moment-stricken eye   her unblinking eye

She had to get down from the blocked train
lick snow from bare cupped hands

taste what had soared into that air
—local cinders, steam of the fast machine

clear her palate with a breath   distinguish
through tumbling whiteness   figures

frozen   figures advancing
weapons at the ready
for the new password

She had to feel her tongue
freeze and burn at once

instrument searching, probing
toward a foreign tongue

2005

HUBBLE PHOTOGRAPHS: AFTER SAPPHO

It should be the most desired sight of all
the person with whom you hope to live and die

walking into a room, turning to look at you, sight for sight
Should be yet I say there is something

more desirable: the ex-stasis of galaxies
so out from us there's no vocabulary

but mathematics and optics
equations letting sight pierce through time

into liberations, lacerations of light and dust
exposed like a body's cavity, violet green livid and venous,
    gorgeous

beyond good and evil as ever stained into dream
beyond remorse, disillusion, fear of death

or life, rage
for order, rage for destruction

—beyond this love which stirs
the air every time she walks into the room

These impersonae, however we call them
won't invade us as on movie screens

they are so old, so new, we are not to them
we look at them or don't from within the milky gauze

of our tilted gazing
but they don't look back and we cannot hurt them

For Jack Litewka

2005

DIRECTOR'S NOTES

You don't want a harsh outcry here
not to violate the beauty yet
dawn unveiling ochre village
but to show coercion
within that beauty, endurance required
Begin with girl
pulling hand over hand on chain
only sound drag and creak
in time it becomes monotonous

then must begin sense of unease produced by monotony
repetitive motion, repetitive sound
resistance, irritation
increasing for the viewers
sense of what are they here for, anyway
dislike of the whole thing how boring to watch

(they aren't used to duration
this was a test)

Keep that dislike that boredom as a value
also as risk
so when bucket finally tinks at rim
they breathe a sigh, not so much relief
as finally grasping
what all this was for

dissolve as she dips from bucket

2005

EVER, AGAIN

Mockingbird shouts *Escape! Escape!*
and would I could   I'd

fly, drive back to that house
up the long hill between queen

anne's lace and common daisyface
shoulder open stuck door

run springwater from kitchen
tap   drench tongue

palate and throat
throw window sashes up screens down

breathe in   mown grass
pine-needle heat

manure, lilac   unpack
brown sacks from the store:

ground meat, buns, tomatoes, one
big onion, milk and orange juice

iceberg lettuce, ranch dressing
potato chips, dill pickles

the *Caledonian-Record*
Portuguese rosé in round-hipped flask

open the box of newspapers by the stove
reread: (Vietnam Vietnam)

Set again on the table
the Olivetti, the stack

of rough yellow typing paper
mark the crashed instant

of one summer's mosquito
on a bedroom door

voices of boys outside
proclaiming twilight and hunger

Pour iced vodka into a shotglass
get food on the table

sitting with those wild heads
over hamburgers, fireflies, music

staying up late with the typewriter
falling asleep with the dead

2006

TELEPHONE RINGING IN THE LABYRINTH

i

You who can be silent in twelve languages
trying to crease again in paling light
the map you unfurled that morning   if

you in your rearview mirror sighted me
rinsing a green glass bowl
by midsummer nightsun in, say, Reykjavík

if at that moment my hand slipped
and that bowl cracked to pieces
and one piece stared at me like a gibbous moon

if its convex reflection caught you walking
the slurried highway shoulder after the car broke down
if such refractions matter

ii

Well, I've held on   peninsula
to continent, climber
to rockface

Sensual peninsula attached so   stroked
by the tides' pensive and moody hands
Scaler into thin air

seen from below as weed or lichen
improvidently fastened
a mat of hair webbed in a bush

A bush ignited   then
consumed
Violent lithography

smolder's legacy on a boulder traced

iii

Image erupts from image
atlas from vagrancy
articulation from mammal howl

strangeness from repetition
even this   default location
surveyed again   one more poem

one more Troy or Tyre or burning tire
seared eyeball genitals
charred cradle

but a different turn   working
this passage of the labyrinth
as laboratory

I'd have entered, searched before
but that ball of thread   that clew
offering an exit choice was no gift at all

iv

I found you by design or
was it your design
or: we were drawn, we drew

Midway in this delicate
negotiation   telephone rings
(Don't stop! . . . they'll call again . . .)

Offstage the fabulous creature scrapes and shuffles
we breathe its heavy dander
I don't care how, if it dies   this is not the myth

No ex/interior: compressed
between my throat
and yours, hilarious oxygen

And, for the record, each did sign
our true names on the register
at the mouth of this hotel

v

I would have wanted to say it
without falling back
on words   Desired not

you so much as your life,
your prevailing   Not for me
but for furtherance   how

you would move
on the horizon   You, the person, you
the particle   fierce and furthering

2006

from

TONIGHT NO POETRY WILL SERVE

(2011)

SERVE (v.t.):
to work for, be a servant to;
to give obedience and reverent honor to;
to fight for; do military or naval service for;
to go through or spend (a term of imprisionment);
to meet the needs of or satisfy the requirements of, be used by;
to deliver (a legal document) as a summons

—*Webster's New World Dictionary*
of the American Language (1964)

WAITING FOR RAIN, FOR MUSIC

Burn me some music   *Send my roots rain*   I'm swept
dry from inside   Hard winds rack my core

A struggle at the roots of the mind   Whoever said
it would go on and on like this

Straphanger swaying inside a runaway car
palming a notebook scribbled in

contraband calligraphy   against the war
poetry wages against itself

•

Once under a shed's eaves
thunder drumming membrane of afternoon
electric scissors slitting the air

thick drops spattering few and far
we could smell it then a long way off

But where's the rain coming to soak this soil

•

Burn me some music   There's a tune
"Neglect of Sorrow"
I've heard it hummed or strummed
my whole life long
in many a corridor

waiting for tomorrow
long after tomorrow
should've come

on many an ear it should have fallen
but the bands were playing so loud

2007

READING THE *ILIAD* (AS IF) FOR THE FIRST TIME

Lurid, garish, gash
rended creature struggles to rise, to
    run with dripping belly
Blood making everything more real
    pounds in the spearthruster's arm as in
the gunman's neck the offhand
moment—Now!—before he
    takes the bastards out

•

Splendor in black and ochre on a grecian urn
    Beauty as truth
The sea as background
    stricken with black long-oared ships
on shore chariots shields greaved muscled legs
    horses rearing   Beauty!   flesh before gangrene

•

Mind-shifting gods rush back and forth   Delusion
a daughter seized by the hair   swung out to bewilder men
Everything here is conflictual and is called man's fate

•

Ugly glory: open-eyed wounds
feed enormous flies
Hoofs slicken on bloodglaze

Horses turn away their heads
weeping equine tears
                    Beauty?
a wall with names of the fallen
from both sides   passionate objectivity

2009

TURBULENCE

There'll be turbulence.   You'll drop
your book to hold your
water bottle steady.   Your
mind, mind has mountains, cliffs of fall
may who ne'er hung there let him
watch the movie.   The plane's
supposed to shudder, shoulder on
like this.   It's built to do that.   You're
designed to tremble too.   Else break
Higher you climb, trouble in mind
lungs labor, heights hurl vistas
Oxygen hangs ready
overhead.   In the event put on
the child's mask first.   Breathe normally

2007

TONIGHT NO POETRY WILL SERVE

Saw you walking barefoot
taking a long look
at the new moon's eyelid

later spread
sleep-fallen, naked in your dark hair
asleep but not oblivious
of the unslept unsleeping
elsewhere

Tonight I think
no poetry
will serve

Syntax of rendition:

verb pilots the plane
adverb modifies action

verb force-feeds noun
submerges the subject
noun is choking
verb   disgraced   goes on doing

now diagram the sentence

2007

AXEL AVÁKAR

[Axel Avákar: fictive poet, counter-muse, brother]

AXEL AVÁKAR

The I you know isn't me, you said, truthtelling liar
My roots are not my chains
And I to you: Whose hands have grown
through mine?   Owl-voiced I cried then: Who?

But yours was the one, the only eye assumed

Did we turn each other into liars?
holding hands with each others' chains?

At last we unhook, dissolve, secrete into islands
—neither a tender place—
yours surf-wrung, kelp-strung
mine locked in black ice on a mute lake

I dug my firepit, built a windbreak,
spread a sheepskin, zoned my telescope lens
to the far ledge of the Milky Way
lay down to sleep out the cold

Daybreak's liquid dreambook:
lines of a long poem pouring down a page
Had I come so far, did I fend so well
only to read your name there, Axel Avákar?

AXEL: BACKSTORY

Steam from a melting glacier

your profile hovering
there   Axel as if we'd lain prone at fifteen
on my attic bedroom floor   elbow to elbow reading
in Baltimorean August-
blotted air

                Axel I'm back to you
brother of strewn books   of late
hours drinking poetry scooped in both hands

Dreamt you into existence, did I, boy-
comrade who would love
                everything I loved

Without my eyelash glittering piercing
sidewise in your eye
where would you have begun, Axel   how
would the wheel-spoke have whirled
your mind?   What word
stirred in your mouth without my
nipples' fierce erection?   our
twixt-and-between

                Between us   yet
my part belonged to me
                and when we parted

I left no part behind   I knew
how to make poetry happen

Back to you Axel through the crackling heavy
salvaged telephone

AXEL, IN THUNDER

Axel, the air's beaten
    like a drumhead here where it seldom thunders

dolphin
        lightning
                leaps

over the bay   surfers flee

    crouching to trucks

climbers hanging
    from pitons in their night hammocks
        off the granite face

wait out an unforetold storm

while somewhere in all weathers you're
    crawling exposed   not by choice   extremist
hell-bent searching your soul

    —O my terrified   my obdurate
my wanderer   keep the trail

I WAS THERE, AXEL

> Pain made her conservative.
> Where the matches touched her flesh, she wears a scar.
>
> —"The Blue Ghazals"

Pain taught her the language
root of *radical*

she walked on knives to gain a voice
fished the lake of lost

messages gulping up
from far below and long ago

needed both arms to haul them in
one arm was tied behind her

the other worked to get it free
it hurt itself because

work hurts   I was there Axel
with her in that boat

working alongside

and my decision was
to be in no other way

a woman

AXEL, DARKLY SEEN, IN A GLASS HOUSE

1

And could it be I saw you
under a roof of glass
in trance

could it be   was passing
by and would translate

too late the strained flicker
of your pupils   your
inert gait   the dark

garb of your reflection
in that translucent place

could be I might have
saved you   still
could   or would   ?

2

Laid my ear to your letter trying to hear
Tongue on your words to taste you there
Couldn't   read what you
*   had never written there*

Played your message over
*   feeling bad*
Played your message over it was all I had
To tell me what and wherefore
*   this is what it said:*

I'm tired of you asking me why
I'm tired of words like the chatter of birds

Give me a pass, let me just get by

3

Back to back our shadows
stalk each other Axel but

not only yours and mine   Thickly lies
the impasto

scrape down far enough you get
the early brushwork   emblems

intimate detail

and scratched lines underneath
—a pictograph

one figure leaning forward
to speak or listen

one figure   backed away
unspeakable

(If that one moved—)

        but the I you knew who made

you once can't save you

my blood won't even match yours

4

"The dead" we say   as if speaking
of "the people" who

gave up on making history
simply to get through

Something dense and null   groan
without echo   underground

and owl-voiced I cry Who
are these dead these people these

lovers who if ever did
listen no longer answer

: *We* :

5

Called in to the dead: *why didn't you write?*
What should I have asked you?

—what would have been the true
unlocking code

if all of them failed—
I've questioned the Book of Questions

studied gyres of steam
twisting from a hot cup
in a cold sunbeam

turned the cards over   lifted the spider's foot
from the mangled hexagon

netted the beaked eel from the river's mouth
asked   and let it go

2007–2008

BALLADE OF THE POVERTIES

There's the poverty of the cockroach kingdom and the rusted
    toilet bowl
The poverty of to steal food for the first time
The poverty of to mouth a penis for a paycheck
The poverty of sweet charity ladling
Soup for the poor who must always be there for that
There's poverty of theory poverty of swollen belly shamed
Poverty of the diploma or ballot that goes nowhere
Princes of predation let me tell you
There are poverties and there are poverties

There's the poverty of cheap luggage bursted open at
immigration
Poverty of the turned head averted eye
The poverty of bored sex of tormented sex
The poverty of the bounced check poverty of the dumpster dive
The poverty of the pawned horn of the smashed reading glasses
The poverty pushing the sheeted gurney the poverty cleaning up
    the puke
The poverty of the pavement artist the poverty passed out on
    pavement
Princes of finance you who have not lain there
There are poverties and there are poverties

There is the poverty of hand-to-mouth and door-to-door
And the poverty of stories patched up to sell there
There's the poverty of the child thumbing the Interstate
And the poverty of the bride enlisting for war
There is the poverty of stones fisted in pocket
And the poverty of the village bulldozed to rubble
There's the poverty of coming home not as you left it
And the poverty of how would you ever end it
Princes of weaponry who have not ever tasted war
There are poverties and there are poverties

There's the poverty of wages wired for the funeral you
Can't get to the poverty of bodies lying unburied
There's the poverty of labor offered silently on the curb
The poverty of the no-contact prison visit
There's the poverty of yard-sale scrapings spread
And rejected the poverty of eviction, wedding bed out on street
Prince let me tell you who will never learn through words
There are poverties and there are poverties

You who travel by private jet like a housefly
Buzzing with the other flies of plundered poverties
Princes and courtiers who will never learn through words
Here's a mirror you can look into: take it: it's yours.

For James and Arlene Scully

2009

EMERGENCY CLINIC

Caustic implacable
poem   unto and contra:

I do not soothe minor
injuries   I do
not offer   I require
                    close history
of the case   apprentice-
ship in past and fresh catastrophe

The skin too quickly scabbed
mutters for my debriding

For every bandaged wound
I'll scrape another   open

I won't smile
                while wiping
your tears
            I do not give
simplehearted   love and nor
allow you simply love me

if you accept   regardless
this will be different

Iodine-dark
poem walking to and fro all night

un-gainly
unreconciled

unto and contra

2008

YOU, AGAIN

Some nights I think you want too much. From me. I didn't ask
to parse again your idioms of littered
parking lots your chain-linked crane-hung sites
limp once more your crime-scene-festooned streets
to buildings I used to live in.   Lose my nerve
at a wrong door on the wrong floor
in search of a time.   The precision of dream is not
such a privilege. I know those hallways tiled in patterns
of oriental rugs those accordion-pleated
elevator gates. Know by heart the chipped
edges on some of those tiles. You who require this
heart-squandering want me wandering you, craving
to press a doorbell hear a lock turn, a bolt slide back
—always too much, over and over back
to the old apartment, wrong again, the key maybe
left with a super in charge of the dream who will not be found

2010

POWERS OF RECUPERATION

i

A woman of the citizen party—*what's that*—
is writing history backward

her body   the chair she sits in
to be abandoned   repossessed

The old, crusading, raping, civil, great, phony, holy, world,
    second world, third world,
    cold, dirty, lost, on drugs,

infectious, maiming, class
war lives on

A done matter she might have thought
ever undone though   plucked

from before her birthyear
and that hyphen coming after

She's old, old, the incendiary
woman

endless beginner

whose warped wraps you shall find in graves
and behind glass   plundered

ii

Streets empty now   citizen rises   shrugging off
her figured shirt   pulls on her dark generic garment   sheds
identity inklings   watch, rings, ear studs
now to pocket her flashlight   her tiny magnet
shut down heater   finger a sleeping cat
lock inner, outer door   insert
key in crevice   listen once twice
to the breath of the neighborhood
take temperature of the signs   a bird
scuffling   a frost settling

*. . . you left that meeting around two a.m.   I thought
someone should walk with you*

Didn't think then I needed that

years ravel out   and now

who'd be protecting whom

I left the key in the old place
in case

iii

Spooky those streets of minds
shuttered against shatter

articulate those walls
pronouncing rage and need

fuck the cops   come jesus
blow me again

Citizen walking catwise
close to the walls

heat of her lungs leaving
its trace upon the air

fingers her tiny magnet
which for the purpose of drawing

particles together will have to do
when as they say the chips are down

iv

Citizen at riverbank   seven bridges
Ministers-in-exile with their aides
limb to limb dreaming underneath

conspiring by definition

Bridges   trajectories arched
in shelter   rendezvous

two banks to every river   two directions
to every bridge
twenty-eight chances

every built thing has its unmeant purpose

v

Every built thing with its unmeant
meaning   unmet purpose

every unbuilt thing

child squatting   civil
engineer   devising

by kerosene flare   in mud
possible tunnels

carves in cornmeal mush   irrigation
canals by index finger

all new learning looks at first
like chaos

the tiny magnet throbs
in citizen's pocket

vi

Bends under the arc walks bent listening for chords and codes
bat-radar-pitched or twanging
off rubber bands and wires tin-can telephony

to scribble testimony by fingernail and echo
her documentary alphabet still evolving

Walks up on the bridge   windwhipped   roof and trajectory
shuddering under her catpaw tread
one of seven

built things holds her suspended
between desolation

and the massive figure on unrest's verge
pondering the unbuilt city

cheek on hand and glowing eyes and
skirted knees apart

2007

from

LATER POEMS

(2013)

ITINERARY

i.

Burnt by lightning   nevertheless
she'll walk this terra infinita

lashes singed on her third eye
searching definite shadows   for an indefinite future

Old shed-boards beaten silvery hang
askew as sheltering
some delicate indefensible existence

Long grasses shiver in a vanished doorway's draft
a place of origins   as yet unclosured and unclaimed

Writing cursive instructions on abounding air

If you arrive with ripe pears, bring a sharpened knife
Bring cyanide with the honeycomb

      call before you come

ii.

Let the face of the bay be violet   black the tumbled torn
kelp necklaces strewn alongshore

Stealthily over time arrives the chokehold
stifling ocean's guttural chorales
                  a tangle
of tattered plastic rags

iii.

In a physical world the great poverty would be
to live insensate   shuttered against the fresh

slash of urine on a wall
low-tidal rumor of a river's yellowed mouth
a tumor-ridden face asleep on a subway train

What would it mean to not possess
a permeable skin
explicit veil to wander in

iv.

A cracked shell crumbles.
Sun moon and salt dissect the faint
last grains

An electrical impulse zings
out   ricochets
in meta-galactic orbits

a streak of nervous energy rejoins the crucible
where origins and endings meld

There was this honey-laden question mark
this thread extracted from the open
throat of existence—Lick it clean!
—let it evaporate—

2011

TRACINGS

This chair delivered yesterday

built for a large heavy man

left me from his estate

lies sidewise legs upturned

He would sit in the chair spooked by his own thoughts

He would say to himself *As the fabric shrinks*

the pattern changes

and forget to write it

He would want to say *The drug that ekes out*

life disenlivens life

I would see words float in the mirror

behind his heaped desk

as thought were smoke

•

The friends I can trust are those who will let me have my death
—traced on a rafter salvaged
from a house marked for demolition

Sky's a mottled marble slab
webs drift off a railing

There were voices here
once, a defiance that still doesn't falter
Imagine a mind overhearing language
split open, uncodified as
yet or never
Imagine a mind sprung open to music
—not the pitiless worm of a tune that won't let you forget it
but a scoreless haunting

2011

ENDPAPERS

i.

If the road's a frayed ribbon strung through dunes
continually drifting over
if the night grew green as sun and moon
changed faces and the sea became
its own unlit unlikely sound
consider yourself lucky to have come
this far   Consider yourself
a trombone blowing unheard
tones   a bass string plucked or locked
down by a hand its face articulated
in shadow, pressed against
a chain-link fence   Consider yourself
inside or outside, where-
ever you were when knotted steel
stopped you short   You can't flow through
as music or
as air

ii.

What holds what binds is breath   is
primal vision in a cloud's eye
is gauze around a wounded head
is bearing a downed comrade out beyond
the numerology of vital signs
into predictless space

iii.

The signature to a life requires
the search for a method
rejection of posturing
trust in the witnesses
a vial of invisible ink
a sheet of paper held steady
after the end-stroke
above a deciphering flame

2011

ADRIENNE RICH'S NOTES
ON THE POEMS

THE DIAMOND CUTTERS

The Snow Queen   Hans Christian Andersen's tale was the point of departure.

The Diamond Cutters   Thirty years later I have trouble with the informing metaphor of this poem. I was trying, in my twenties, to write about the craft of poetry. But I was drawing, quite ignorantly, on the long tradition of domination, according to which the precious resource is yielded up into the hands of the dominator as if by a natural event. The enforced and exploited labor of actual Africans in actual diamond mines was invisible to me and, therefore, invisible in the poem, which does not take responsibility for its own metaphor. I note this here because this kind of metaphor is still widely accepted, and I still have to struggle against it in my work. (1984)

SNAPSHOTS OF A DAUGHTER-IN-LAW

Snapshots of a Daughter-in-Law   Part 4: "My Life had stood—a Loaded Gun," Emily Dickinson, *Complete Poems*, ed. T. H. Johnson, 1960, p. 369.

Part 7: The lines in Part 7 beginning "To have in this uncertain world some stay" were written by Mary Wollstonecraft in *Thoughts on the Education of Daughters* (London, 1787).

Part 8: "Vous mourez toutes à quinze ans," from Diderot's *Lettres à Sophie Volland*, quoted by Simone de Beauvoir in *Le Deuxième Sexe*, vol. II, pp. 123–24.

Part 10: Cf. *Le Deuxième Sexe*, vol. II, p. 574: ". . . elle arrive du fond des ages, de Thèbes, de Minos, de Chichen Itza; et elle est aussi le totem planté au coeur de la brousse africaine; c'est un helicoptère et c'est un oiseau; et voilà la plus grande merveille: sous ses cheveux peints le bruissement des feuillages devient une pensée et des paroles s'échappent de ses seins."

("She comes from the remotest ages, from Thebes, Minos, Chichén Itzá; and she is also a totem planted in the heart of the African jungle; she is a helicopter and she is a bird; and here is the greatest wonder: beneath her painted hair, the rustling of leaves becomes a thought and words escape from her breasts." *The Second Sex*, translated by Constance Borde and Sheila Malovany-Chevallier, Vintage Feminism Short Edition.)

NECESSITIES OF LIFE

In the Woods   The first line is borrowed and translated from the Dutch poet J. C. Bloem.

"I Am in Danger—Sir—"   See Thomas Johnson and Theodora Ward, eds., *The Letters of Emily Dickinson*, vol. 2 (Cambridge, Mass.: Harvard University Press, 1958), p. 409. (The poem was first published as an epigraph to *Emily Dickinson: The Mind of the Poet* by Albert J. Gelpi [Cambridge, Mass.: Harvard University Press, 1965] under the title "E.")

LEAFLETS

Orion   One or two phrases suggested by Gottfried Benn's essay "Artists and Old Age," in *Primal Vision: Selected Writings*, ed. E. B. Ashton (New York: New Directions, 1960).

To Frantz Fanon   Revolutionary philosopher; studied medicine at the Sorbonne; worked as a psychiatrist in Algeria during the Franco-Algerian war; died of cancer at thirty-six. Author of *The Wretched of the Earth; Toward the African Revolution; Black Skin, White Masks; A Dying Colonialism.*

Leaflets   Part 2: "The love of a fellow-creature in all its fullness consists simply in the ability to say to him: 'What are you going through?'" (Simone Weil, *Waiting for God*).

Ghazals (Homage to Ghalib)   This poem began to be written after I read Aijaz Ahmad's literal English versions of the Urdu poetry of Mirza Ghalib (1797–1869). While the structure and metrics of the classical *ghazal* form used by Ghalib are much stricter than mine, I adhered to his use of a minimum five couplets to a *ghazal*, each couplet being autonomous and independent of the others. The continuity and unity flow from the associations and images playing back and forth among the couplets in any single *ghazal*. The poems are dated as I wrote them, during a month in the summer of 1968. Although I was a contributor to Ahmad's *The Ghazals of Ghalib* (New York: Columbia University Press, 1971), the *ghazals* here are not translations, but original poems.

My *ghazals* are personal and public, American and twentieth-century; but they owe much to the presence of Ghalib in my mind: a poet self-educated and profoundly learned, who owned no property and borrowed his books, writing in an age of political and cultural break-up (1993).

POEMS

From an Old House in America   Part 4: The first line is borrowed from Emily Brontë's poem "Stanzas."

Part 7: Many African women went into labor and gave birth on the slave-ships of the Middle Passage, chained for the duration of the voyage to the dying or the dead.

Part 11: *Datura* is a poisonous hallucinogenic weed with a spiky green pod and a white flower; also known as jimson-weed, or deadly nightshade.

A WILD PATIENCE HAS TAKEN ME THIS FAR

Integrity   To my knowledge, this word was first introduced in a feminist context by Janice Raymond in her essay "The Illusion of Androgyny," *Quest: A Feminist Quarterly* 2, no. I (Summer 1975).

For Ethel Rosenberg   Phrases italicized in Part 3, line 6, are from Robert Coover's novel *The Public Burning* (New York: Viking, 1977).

The Spirit of Place Part III: Italicized passages are from Thomas Johnson and Theodora Ward, eds., *The Letters of Emily Dickinson* (Cambridge, Mass.: Harvard University Press, 1958), specifically, from Letter 154 to Susan Gilbert (June 1854) and Letter 203 to Catherine Scott Anthon Turner (March 1859).

YOUR NATIVE LAND, YOUR LIFE

Sources The phrase "an end to suffering" was evoked by a sentence in Nadine Gordimer's *Burger's Daughter*: "No one knows where the end of suffering will begin."

North American Time Section IX: Julia de Burgos (1914–1953), Puerto Rican poet and revolutionary who died on the streets of New York City.

Dreams Before Waking "Hasta tu país cambió. Lo has cambiado tú mismo" ("Even your country has changed. You yourself have changed it"). These lines, from Morejón's "Elogio de la Dialéctica," and Georgina Herrera's poem "Como Presentaciön, Como Disculpa" can be found in Margaret Randall, ed., *Breaking the Silences: 20th Century Poetry by Cuban Women* (1982). Pulp Press, 3868 MPO, Vancouver, Canada V6B 3Z3.

Yom Kippur 1984 The epigraph and quoted lines from Robinson Jeffers come from *The Women at Point Sur and Other Poems* (New York: Liveright, 1977).

Contradictions Section 16: See Elizabeth Bishop, *The Complete Poems 1927–1979* (New York: Farrar, Straus & Giroux, 1983), p. 173.

Section 26: See Cynthia Ozick, *Art and Ardor* (New York: Farrar, Straus & Giroux, 1984), p. 255: "the glorious So What: the life-cry."

TIME'S POWER

Living Memory "it was pick and shovel work . . .": quoted from *Wally Hunt's Vermont* (Brownington, Vt.: Orleans County Historical Society, 1983).

An Atlas of the Difficult World   Part V: "over the chained bay waters": From Hart Crane, "To Brooklyn Bridge," in *The Poems of Hart Crane*, ed. Marc Simon (New York and London: Liveright, 1989; poem originally published in 1930).

"There are roads to take when you think of your country": From Muriel Rukeyser, *U.S. 1* (New York: Covici Friede, 1938); see also Muriel Rukeyser, *The Collected Poems* (New York: McGraw-Hill, 1978).

"I don't want to know how he tracked them": On May 13, 1988, Stephen Roy Carr shot and killed Rebecca Wight, one of two lesbians camping on the Appalachian Trail in Pennsylvania. Her lover, Claudia Brenner, suffered five bullet wounds. She dragged herself two miles along the trail to a road, where she flagged a car to take her to the police. In October of that year, Carr was found guilty of first-degree murder and sentenced to life in prison without parole. During the legal proceedings, it became clear that Carr had attacked the women because they were lesbians. See *Gay Community News* (August 7 and November 11, 1988).

Part VI: "Hatred of England smouldering like a turf-fire": See Nella Braddy, *Anne Sullivan Macy: The Story behind Helen Keller* (Garden City, N.Y.: Doubleday, Doran & Company, 1933), p. 13.

"Meat three times a day": See Frank Murray, "The Irish and Afro-Americans in U.S. History," *Freedomways: A Quarterly Review of the Freedom Movement* 22, no. 1 (1982): 22.

Part X: The passages in italics are quoted from *Soledad Brother: The Prison Letters of George Jackson* (New York: Bantam, 1970), pp. 24, 26, 93, 245.

Eastern War Time   Part 10: "A coat is not a piece of cloth only": See Barbara Myerhoff, *Number Our Days* (New York: Simon & Schuster, 1978), p. 44. Myerhoff quotes Shmuel Goldman, immigrant Socialist garment-worker: "It is not the way of a Jew to make his work like there was no human being to suffer when it's done badly. A coat is not a piece of cloth only. The tailor is connected to the one who wears it and he should not forget it."

Tattered Kaddish "The Reapers of the Field are the Comrades, masters of this wisdom, because Malkhut is called the Apple Field, and She grows sprouts of secrets and new meanings of Torah. Those who constantly create new interpretations of Torah are the ones who reap Her" (Moses Cordovero, Or ha-Hammah on Zohar III, 106a). See Barry W. Holtz, ed., *Back to the Sources: Reading the Classic Jewish Texts* (New York: Summit, 1984), p. 305.

DARK FIELDS OF THE REPUBLIC

What Kind of Times Are These The title is from Bertolt Brecht's poem "An Die Nachgeborenen" ("For Those Born Later"): "What kind of times are these / When it's almost a crime to talk about trees / Because it means keeping still about so many evil deeds?" (For the complete poem, in a different translation, see John Willett and Ralph Manheim, eds., *Bertolt Brecht, Poems 1913–1956* [New York: Methuen, 1976], pp. 318–20.)

"our country moving closer to its own truth and dread . . .": echoes Osip Mandelstam's 1921 poem that begins "I was washing outside in the darkness" and ends "The earth's moving closer to truth and to dread." (Clarence Brown and W. S. Merwin, trans., *Osip Mandelstam: Selected Poems* [New York: Atheneum, 1974], p. 40.) Mandelstam was forbidden to publish, then exiled and sentenced to five years of hard labor for a poem caricaturing Stalin; he died in a transit camp in 1938.

"To be human, said Rosa . . .": Rosa Luxemburg (1871–1919) was a Polish-born middle-class Jew. Early in her abbreviated life she entered the currents of European socialist revolutionary thinking and action. She became one of the most influential and controversial figures in the social-democratic movements of Eastern Europe and Germany. Besides her political essays, she left hundreds of vivid letters to friends and comrades. Imprisoned during World War I for her strongly internationalist and anticapitalist beliefs, she was murdered in Berlin in 1919 by right-wing soldiers, with the passive collusion of a faction from her own party. Her body was thrown into a canal.

On December 28, 1916, from prison, she wrote a New Year letter to friends she feared were both backsliding and complaining: "Then see to it that you remain a *Mensch*! [Yiddish/German for human being] . . . Being a *Mensch* means happily throwing one's life 'on fate's great scale' if necessary, but, at the same time, enjoying every bright day and every beautiful cloud. Oh, I can't write you a prescription for being a *Mensch*. I only know how one is a *Mensch*, and you used to know it too when we went walking for a few hours in the Südende fields with the sunset's red light falling on the wheat. The world is so beautiful even with all its horrors." (*The Letters of Rosa Luxemburg*, ed., trans., and with an introduction by Stephen Eric Bronner [Atlantic Highlands, N.J.: Humanities Press, 1993], p. 173.)

Calle Visión   Calle Visión is the name of a road in the southwestern United States—literally, "Vision Street."

"that tells the coming of the railroad": "With the coming of the railroad, new materials and pictorial designs and motifs, including trains themselves, appeared in Navaho weaving (ca. 1880)." (From the Museum of Indian Arts and Culture, Museum of New Mexico, Santa Fe.)

"a place not to live but to die in": See Sir Thomas Browne, *Religio Medici* (1635): "For the World, I count it not an Inn, but an Hospital; and a place not to live, but to dye in." (*Religio Medici and Other Writings by Sir Thomas Browne* [London: Everyman's Library, J. M. Dent, 1947], p. 83.)

"Have you ever worked around metal? . . .": From a questionnaire filled out before undergoing a magnetic resonance imaging (MRI) scan.

"The world is falling down. . . .": From the song "The World Is Falling Down," composed by Abbey Lincoln, sung by her on the Verve recording of the same title, 1990 (Moseka Music BMI).

"And the fire shall try. . . .": I Corinthians 3:13: "Every man's work shall be made manifest . . . and the fire shall try every man's work of what sort it is." Used by Studs Terkel as an epigraph to his *Working* (New York: Pantheon, 1974).

Late Ghazal See "Ghazals (Homage to Ghalib)" on pages 75–77 and "The Blue Ghazals" on pages 88–92. See also Aijaz Ahmad, ed., *Ghazals of Ghalib* (New York: Columbia University Press, 1971).

MIDNIGHT SALVAGE

Camino Real "Can you afford not to make / the magical study / which happiness is?": From Charles Olson, "Variations Done for Gerald Van der Wiele," in *Charles Olson, Selected Poems*, ed. Robert Creeley (Berkeley: University of California Press, 1997), p. 83.

"George Oppen to June Degnan: . . .": See George Oppen, *The Selected Letters of George Oppen*, ed. Rachel Blau DuPlessis (Durham, N.C.: Duke University Press, 1990), p. 212.

FOX

Noctilucent Clouds "Several times in the last few months, observers in the lower 48 have seen 'noctilucent clouds,' which develop about 50 miles above the earth's surface—clouds so high that they reflect the sun's rays long after nightfall. . . . [G]lobal warming seems to be driving them toward the equator. . . . In retrospect it will be clear." Bill McKibben, "Indifferent to a Planet in Pain," *New York Times*, September 4, 1999, sec. A.

Terza Rima Section 3: *Vivo nel non volare* . . . : "I live in the failed will / of the post-war time / loving the world I hate"—Pier Paolo Pasolini, "Le Ceneri di Gramsci," in Lawrence R. Smith, ed. and trans., *The New Italian Poetry, 1945 to the Present* (Berkeley: University of California Press, 1981), pp. 80–81. See also Pier Paolo Pasolini, *Poems*, selected and trans. Norman MacAfee and Luciano Martinengo (London: John Calder, 1982), pp. 10–11.

Waiting for You at the Mystery Spot " 'The *mystai* streamed' toward [the Telestrion]." C. Kerényi, *Eleusis*, trans. Ralph Manheim, Bollingen series 65, vol. 4 (New York: Bollingen Foundation/Pantheon, 1967), p. 82.

Tell Me   "remembered if outlived / as freezing": Emily Dickinson, *The Complete Poems*, ed. Thomas H. Johnson (Boston: Little, Brown, 1960), no. 341.

"harrowed in defeats of language": Michael Heller, "Sag Harbor, Whitman, As If an Ode," in *Wordflow: New and Selected Poems* (Jersey City, N.J.: Talisman House, 1997), p. 129.

"in history to my barest marrow": *Black Salt: Poems by Édouard Glissant*, trans. Betsy Wing (Ann Arbor: University of Michigan Press, 1998), p. 33.

This evening let's   "friendship is not a tragedy": See June Jordan, "Civil Wars" (1980), in *Some of Us Did Not Die: New and Selected Essays* (New York: Basic Books, 2002), p. 267.

Transparencies   "we are truely sorry . . .": Clyde Haberman, "Palestinians Reclaim Their Town after Israelis Withdraw," *New York Times*, August 31, 2001, p. A6.

TELEPHONE RINGING IN THE LABYRINTH

Calibrations   Landstuhl: American military hospital in Germany.

"You go to war with the army you have." U.S. Secretary of Defense Donald Rumsfeld, December 2004.

Hubble Photographs: After Sappho   For Sappho, see *Greek Lyric, I: Sappho, Alcaeus*, trans. David A. Campbell, Loeb Classical Library 142 (Cambridge, Mass.: Harvard University Press, 1982–), fragment 16, pp. 66–67: "Some say a host of cavalry, others of infantry, and others of ships, is the most beautiful thing on the black earth, but I say it is whatsoever a person loves. . . . I would rather see her lovely walk and the bright sparkle of her face than the Lydians' chariots and armed infantry."

TONIGHT NO POETRY WILL SERVE

Waiting for Rain, for Music   "*Send my roots rain*": Gerard Manley Hopkins, *Gerard Manley Hopkins: Selections*, ed. Catherine Phillips, The Oxford Authors (New York: Oxford University Press, 1986), p. 183.

"A struggle at the roots of the mind": Raymond Williams, *Marxism and Literature* (Oxford, UK: Oxford University Press, 1977), p. 212.

Reading the Iliad *(As If) for the First Time*   "For those dreamers who considered that force, thanks to progress, would soon be a thing of the past, the *Iliad* could appear as an historical document; for others, whose powers of recognition are more acute and who perceive force, today as yesterday, at the very center of human history, the *Iliad* is the purest and the loveliest of mirrors": Simone Weil, *The Iliad; or, The Poem of Force* (1940), trans. Mary McCarthy (Wallingford, Pa.: Pendle Hill, 1956), p. 3.

"Delusion / a daughter": See Homer, *The Iliad*, trans. Richmond Lattimore (Chicago: University of Chicago Press, 1951), pp. 394–95, bk. 19, lines 91–130.

"Horses turn away their heads / weeping": Homer, pp. 365–66, bk. 17, lines 426–40.

Turbulence   "O the mind, mind has mountains, cliffs of fall / Frightful, sheer . . . Hold them cheap / May he who ne'er hung there": Gerard Manley Hopkins, *Gerard Manley Hopkins: Selections*, ed. Catherine Phillips, The Oxford Authors (New York: Oxford University Press, 1986), p. 167.

I was there, Axel   "The Blue Ghazals." See "The Blue Ghazals," pages 88–92.

Ballade of the Poverties   This revival of an old form owes inspiration to François Villon, *The Poems of François Villon*, ed. and trans. Galway Kinnell (Boston: Houghton Mifflin, 1977).

Powers of Recuperation   "the massive figure on unrest's verge." See *Melencolia I*, a 1514 engraving by Albrecht Dürer. The "I" is thought to refer to "Melencolia Imaginativa," one of three types of melancholy described by Heinrich Cornelius Agrippa (1486–1535).

INDEX OF TITLES AND
FIRST LINES

ABOUT THE EDITORS

Albert Gelpi is the William Robertson Coe Professor of American Literature, emeritus, at Stanford University. His books include *Emily Dickinson: The Mind of the Poet*, *Living in Time: The Poetry of C. Day Lewis*, and a trilogy on the historical/critical development of an American poetic tradition: *The Tenth Muse*, *A Coherent Splendor*, and *American Poetry after Modernism: The Power of the Word*. Among the other volumes he has edited are *Wallace Stevens: The Aesthetics of Modernism*, *The Wild God of the World: A Robinson Jeffers Reader*, and (with Robert J. Bertholf) *The Letters of Robert Duncan and Denise Levertov*.

Barbara Charlesworth Gelpi is a professor of English, emerita, at Stanford University, where she taught nineteenth-century English literature and feminist theory. She has written *Dark Passages: The Decadent Consciousness in Victorian Literature* and *Shelley's Goddess: Maternity, Language, and Subjectivity*. She has coedited *Victorian Women: A Documentary Account of Women's Lives in Nineteenth-Century England, France, and the United States*, edited *Signs: A Journal of Women in Culture and Society* from 1980 to 1985, and was director of the Clayman Institute for the Study of Women and Gender at Stanford from 2002 to 2004.

Brett C. Millier is the Reginald L. Cook Professor of American Literature at Middlebury College. She is the author of *Elizabeth Bishop: Life and the Memory of It* and *Flawed Light: American Women Poets and Alcohol*. She is also associate editor of *The Columbia History of American Poetry*.

The editors have also edited the second Norton Critical Edition of *Adrienne Rich: Poetry and Prose*.